"Ritamary Bradley's prayerful encounter with Dame Julian will provide more spiritual depth to a text which already has the deserved reputation as one of the classics of Christian spirituality. Highly regarded as a Julian scholar, she now shows her capacity to respond to the Divine Revelations from the perspective of prayer. We are all in Bradley's debt."

Lawrence S. Cunningham
University of Notre Dame

"The invitation tendered in *Praying with Julian of Norwich* consists, first, in a graceful rendering of the medieval English and then a well-crafted series of commentaries on portions of her *Shewings*. This is a book not to be read through—although that can be done—but for use and re-use as one attempts to pray. No shallow 'spiritual reading,' this is depth of spirit compounded by depth."

Gerard S. Sloyan
Author, *Jesus in Focus*

"This book on Julian of Norwich is unique in that it mines *A Revelation of Love* for what it can teach us about prayer. If interested in Julian, in the theory of prayer, or in praying, there is something here for you. Commentary is offered to clarify Julian's intent and to deepen her message for the reader. This book is filled with simplicity and rich complexity."

Dana Greene
Author, *Evelyn Underhill: Artist of the Infinite Life*

"Bradley helps today's seekers draw upon Julian's wisdom as they make their own ways into oneness with the Divine. Whether they choose to pursue this challenge in solitude (as Julian did), or as part of a prayer group, readers will find their paths illumined by Julian and Bradley: two women who have heard God and call us to do the same."

Margaret Susan Thompson, Ph.D.
Syracuse University

"This book is ideal for individual use or for group reading and reflection. It enables Julian to lead her listeners into the deeper wisdom of Christ and the Spirit."

The (Dublin) Irish Catholic

"Here we have a late 20th-century commentary by Ritamary Bradley on Julian's Revelations that shows each of these gifted contemplative women to be attentive to the world as-it-is, able to fix the turbulence in each instance with a gauge of compassionate understanding that ultimately restores the possibility of peace, and joins the medieval to the modern moment in ways that astonish as well as reassure us: *All will be well....*"

Dolores W. Frese
University of Notre Dame

"Just as Julian of Norwich spoke to her 'even Christians' of the 14th century, so, too, does she speak to them today, mediated by Ritamary Bradley's artful presentation of Julian's text and her own deft commentaries. This book provides not only a timely presentation of Julian's voice, but also invites each reader to reflect on the resonances of her message."

Sandra McEntire
Rhodes College

"Ritamary Bradley and Julian make a simpatico pair, one way of knowing meshed with the other in harmony. The 20th-century woman and the 14th-century anchoress have a conversation on these pages that we can hear. Bradley does not so much speak for Julian as speak along with her, and also selects for some of the commentaries beautifully apt illustrations from other writers. So we are pleased to listen to these strong voices of loving thought. "

Elizabeth Psakis Armstrong
Editor, *Mystics Quarterly*

"Books about Julian are, perhaps, in danger of becoming an industry, but this latest volume by the noted scholar Ritamary Bradley is a particularly good example of how to mediate good scholarship in digestible form. It is a book for devotional use or group reflection rather than for academic study."

Philip Sheldrake, S.J.

"*Praying with Julian of Norwich* takes selected passages and reflects on them. Deep but accessible. Easily one of the best of the many books about Julian."

Norwich (England) Diocesan News

Praying with
Julian of Norwich

Selections from "A Revelation of Love"
with Commentary

Ritamary Bradley

TWENTY-THIRD PUBLICATIONS
Mystic, Connecticut 06355

North American Edition 1995

Originally published in 1994 as *Not for the Wise* by Darton, Longman and Todd Ltd. London, England.

Twenty-Third Publications
185 Willow Street
P.O. Box 180
Mystic, CT 06355
(203) 536-2611
800-321-0411

ISBN 0-89622-601-8
Library of Congress Catalog Card Number 94-60353
Printed in the U.S.A.

Acknowledgments

Scripture quotations are taken from the *New American Bible*, copyright © 1986 by the Confraternity of Christian Doctrine, 3111 Fourth Street N.E., Washington, D. C., and are used with permission. All rights reserved.

Thanks are due to the following for permission to quote copyright material: Joseph Cunneen, editor, for quotations from Leo J. O'Donovan, S.J., in *Cross Currents*, College of New Rochelle, New Rochelle, N.Y.; Robert J. Daly, S.J., editor, for quotations from Gregory Baum in *Theological Studies*, Boston College, Chestnut Hill, Mass.; Exeter University Press and Marion Glasscoe for permission to use the Middle English text, Julian of Norwich, *A Revelation of Love* (1986), Marion Glasscoe (ed.), as a basis for translations; the Hibbert Trust for quotations from Bede Griffiths, the Hibbert Lecture 1989, reprinted in part in *Bulletin of the North American Board for East-West Dialogue* (now *Monastic Interreligious Dialogue*); Janet Morely for a selection from *All Desires Known* (SPCK 1992); Sheed and Ward for lines from *Selected Poetry of Jessica Powers*, Regina Siegfried and Robert Morneau, editors (1989); James Somerville, editor, and Anne Adkins, author, for quotations from *The Roll*, Pfafftown, North Carolina; Source Books for lines from Edwina Gately, *Songs for a Laywoman* (1986).

Thanks are also due to St. Ambrose University for the use of computer and copier services in the preparation of the typescript.

Contents

Introduction

Methods and theories of prayer abound today. Books, tapes, conferences, and retreats focus on this interest and nourish the desire of many to grow in a contemplative life. Likewise, much reading and reflection center on the wise words of Mother Julian (1342–c.1420). This book, *Praying with Julian of Norwich*, brings these two interests together for both individuals and groups.

Process

In the traditions of methods of prayer, this book is particularly well adapted to the practice called *lectio divina* in the Rule of St. Benedict. Aiming at savor, not science, the monks united reading, meditation, and prayer, all oriented toward life rather than toward abstract knowledge. The whole person engages in this effort, particularly through the memory. Though commonly based on the Scriptures, the method also applies to other writings growing out of the experiences of people of virtue and prayer.

Passages on prayer from Julian's *A Revelation of Love* are the core of this book. Short reflections, called Commentary, follow the selected texts. The prayer texts may profitably be read aloud, or at least in a low tone, and recited rhythmically like a chant, where possible. Some parts are effectively read in chorus, or by alternate voices. For this reason, Julian's text in the following pages is broken into sense lines, which hold the attention and halt the progressive leaping ahead to the completed idea, with only the intellect engaged. In this way we see, hear, think, and imagine in a single activity. The method is like that used today for learning a language, aimed at imprinting the words on body and psyche.

But becoming familiar with the language is not an end in itself. It is rather a means for taking in the content of the words. This procedure is followed by drawing out all the nutrients of the text, in a process called by the metaphor of rumination, or savoring.

Such repeated experiences, lived with the full energy of intention, are expected to take root in the whole person so as to bear fruit later. One becomes "seeded" with holy words, which grow into holy actions.

A further means for penetrating all levels of consciousness with the texts is by using each word to evoke other passages where this same word is used. In the reading of the Scriptures, such a word as bread, for example, would call up the memory of the manna in the desert, the meaning of Bethlehem as "house of bread," the miracle of the loaves, the Satanic temptation inviting Christ to "change these stones into bread"; the trial of the disciples when Christ called his flesh, bread to be eaten; the Eucharist itself as the bread of life; the coming rule of God figured as yeast in a loaf of bread; and especially the need to share bread with the hungry whom we will recognize at the judgment as Christ himself. Thus a word is not an abstract concept, but a knitting together of meanings and experiences into a fabric enlivened with feelings, memories, and desires.

In line with this process of assimilating a text through focusing on key words, important phrases and words in Julian's prayer passages have been highlighted (with italics). An allusion to one of them spontaneously gives rise to remembering a multitude of associations. Thus rumination facilitates reminiscence. These are not just "idea" words, but words woven by Julian into the living pattern of her teaching on prayer. They are to be approached as far as possible with the imagination, and their meaning filled out by the different contexts in which they occur. The commentaries that follow the texts are intended both to clarify meanings and to help in the total process, which individuals or groups will pursue in their own way.

In these passages Julian shares with us what she learned about prayer in visions, in reflective reasoning, and in "spiritual sights." In other words, these texts are the fruit of her rumination on the pictures, words, and spiritual overflow of the "Showings," which are sixteen closely related experiences of enlightenment that came to her after an illness that nearly ended her life.

She teaches us how to practice prayer, to lead a prayerful life, and to receive, when grace sends them, mystical gifts of a contemplative nature.

In a way, of course, what Julian offers is not a method, in the sense of repeated or directed exercises designed to bring about measurable effects. It does not guarantee even transcendental experiences, the acquisition of which, it seems, can be taught. Rather, she leaves the way open for God to teach each of us according to our capacity to receive. What we are to bring to these divine lessons Julian explains in the passages on prayer.[1]

Overview

Julian of Norwich, a teacher of prayer, was an anchoress, one given to religious seclusion and prayer, in 14th-century England. She weaves her teachings into the account of her Showings. In these experiences Julian saw several scenes from the passion of Christ. She also understood that where Christ is, there is the Trinity, whose presence is manifested as joy. God is disclosed as both awe-inspiring and familiar, or, as she says, courteous and commonplace. Throughout, Julian grows in love for her "even-Christians" (Julian's term for the community of Christians without distinction of clergy, religious, and laity), to whom she is bound in her oneness with Christ. The goodness of God, active in all that has been made, consoled her, but the problem of sin troubled her. Yet she came to understand that, despite sin, humanity is called to partnership with God in a great deed that will make all things well. This deed, though it is now in the making, remains a mystery.

A parable of a lord and a servant helped her to see the necessity of sin and to begin to understand God's unbroken love. The lesson of the parable rests on our unity with Christ. In the depth of our soul we share his life in the Trinity; in his becoming human, we are bound to him and to one another like kin. The image of God and Christ as mother exemplifies this unity. In sum, the Showings are about love: The inner life of God is love; God is love, in making a home in humanity; and by love we are in partnership with God in charity among ourselves and in cooperating in the deed that will make all things well.

The visions she reports took only a few hours. She wrote a short text first, while the Showings were fresh in her memory. Then she devoted some twenty years to reasoning about them, and to drawing from them ever deeper insights grounded in her faith. These are the energies from which we, too, can become more enriched in the practice of prayer.

Praying with Julian of Norwich builds on Julian's words directed to the subject of prayer. Her teachings are examined in five related parts, which as a whole constitute her own experiences and growth in understanding. She tells us 1) of the beginnings of her prayer; 2) of seeing that the focus of prayer is God's goodness, which is the Trinity; 3) of understanding that Christ is the center of prayer; 4) of understanding, further, that Christ is the foundation—the source—of prayer; 5) and of knowing, in the heights and depths of her own heart, God's mystical self-disclosure.

A Prelude As a prelude, we listen to how the Holy Spirit taught Julian to gain the most from ruminating on spiritual matters. This inner teaching comes to her in the context of the parable of the lord and the servant, which she regards as an answer to her concerns over sin. She learns to focus on the truth that Christ has become one with all who accept his saving gifts. There is no longer domination, only friendship. This is the same teaching that Christ reveals through the Scriptures when he says, "I am the vine; you are the branches." We do not pray alone.

Beginnings On May 8, 1373, Julian is beset by an illness so severe that she thought she was going to die. On the fourth day she receives the rites of the church and resigns herself to death, though she would like to live to love God for a longer time. As she looks straight up to heaven, hoping thereby to receive God's mercy, she assents to the attending priest's invitation to fix her eyes instead on the image of the cross. This initiates a series of sixteen Showings, as she calls them, which will be the subject of her book. Then she recalls that in her youth she had asked three gifts of God: 1) To have a vivid, lasting awareness of the passion; 2) to come to the brink of death at thirty years of age, so that she might be jolted into leading a better life; and 3) to have three deep dispositions that suited her spiritual state. The first two "wounds," as she calls them, were contrition for her sins and compassion for the suffering Christ. The third was a longing for God, rooted in her nature and made firm by her own fixed intention (Chapters 1 and 2).

The Focus of Prayer: The Goodness of God Then she tells what she sees, what she thinks about it, and what insights sink into her soul. Her first Showings are of the passion and are grounded in some of the principal foundations of faith. These provide a focus for her prayer. At the outset she learns that her prayer should be directed "to the goodness of God" (first Showing, Chapter 6). Troubled by questions about sin, she is shown that the power of the passion subdues the fiend, who will try to blunt and destroy her Showing. In the second Showing (Chapter 10), she learns that seeking and finding God are equally good. The third Showing (Chapter 11) contains her first lesson in seeing God in all that is.

Christ the Center of Prayer After having contemplated another scene from the passion (fourth Showing, Chapter 12), Julian introduces the prayer of listening (fifth Showing, Chapter 13). This is a prelude to an understanding of heaven under the image of a festivity in which Christ is a host among friends (sixth Showing, Chapter 14). This is followed by a feeling of emptiness in which she teaches by example how to conduct oneself at such times (seventh Showing, Chapter 15). She perseveres in choosing Jesus for her heaven in the face of a temptation to look for God without embracing the cross. She learns of the all-pervasive presence of the risen Christ (eighth

Showing, Chapters 19-20). This insight is expanded into seeing that although the passion took place in the past, the love that it expressed has neither beginning nor end (ninth Showing, Chapters 22-23). This love of Christ manifests the Trinity, and is an assurance that true prayer is always answered (tenth Showing, Chapter 24).

Julian reveals, however, that her repeated prayer for a visible sight of Mary was not granted (eleventh Showing, Chapter 25). In the most sublime of her interchanges with God in prayer, Julian tells us how the risen Christ animates all that we rightfully love and desire (twelfth Showing, Chapter 26). The long thirteenth Showing (Chapters 27-40) is interspersed with wisdom about the practical experience of prayer and difficulties in its practice.

Christ the Foundation of Prayer The fourteenth Showing (Chapters 41-43) hinges on Julian's analysis of the two conditions for prayer, as summarized in her overview of the whole revelation; it contains a definition that she explains. Subsequent reflections (Chapters 44-63) include the parable of the lord and the servant (Chapter 51). The fifteenth Showing (Chapters 64-65) is directed primarily to all who aspire to make prayer, as Julian herself practiced and taught it, the center of their lives.

The Height and Depth of Julian's Prayer The sixteenth Showing, which is the revelation as a whole understood in the interrelation of its parts, reteaches the lessons on prayer in greater depth (Chapters 67-68). This is preceded and followed (in Chapters 66 and 69) by an account of demonic temptations. In the closing chapters (70-86) we learn of Julian's mystical encounters with God.

Such is the dynamic universe of prayer that Julian invites us to enter.

Prelude
From the Parable of the Lord and the Servant

For twenty years, less three months, after the time of this Showing [of the parable of the Lord and the Servant] I had inward teaching, as I shall explain:

For your part you should carefully go over all the details and circumstances that were shown in the parable, even though you find them cloudy and unclear.

I gave willing assent, with great desire, reflecting inwardly with full deliberation on all the points and details that had been shown beforehand, as far as my mind and understanding would permit.

I began by beholding the Lord and the Servant, by noting the Lord's manner of sitting, the place where he sat, the color of his clothing, and its style, his outward expression, and his inner nobility and goodness.

Then I deliberated on the Servant, on how and where he stood, on his kind of clothing, along with its color and style, on how he looked outwardly, and on his inner goodness and his good will.

I understood that the Lord who sat solemnly in rest and peace is God,

The Servant who stood before the Lord I understood to be Adam—that is to say, a particular man was meant at that time.

His falling was to show how God looks on our falling, for in the sight of God we are all one; all of us are one [body], and one [body] is all of us.

Chapter 51

Beginnings

The Texts on Prayer

Our Lord is the ground of our petitioning.
  Herein were seen two properties:

> —the one requires that prayer be *right* in itself;
> —and the other requires of us firm *trust.*

God wants both of these to be equally generous.
"Thus our prayers please you;
And *of your goodness* you fulfill them."

Chapter 1

COMMENTARY

This succinct statement on prayer unfolds in the course of the Showings in two ways:

—in Julian's own experience, as she prays;
—in her application to prayer of what the Showings reveal.

Though much of the fourteenth Showing is given over explicitly to the teaching on prayer, what goes before and what comes after prepare for and confirm this direct teaching.

Though Julian does not here summarize the parable of the lord and the servant, it is also a part of the fourteenth Showing. That central parable helps resolve many problems about rightful and trusting prayer. It may be useful to read that parable again before reviewing Julian's overall reflections on prayer. The parable is not contained in the Short Version of her Showings—because at that time she did not understand it. Even in the Long Version she labels it as somewhat unclear. (See Prelude and Julian's Chapters 51-52.) She reflected on it for many years before she felt ready to reveal it to those she teaches.

Some Prayer in Youth

These revelations were shown to a simple creature . . . in the year of our Lord, 1373, on the eighth of May. This creature had earlier desired three gifts from God:

—*The first* was to have a right sense of the passion.
—*The second* was to have a bodily sickness while still young
   —at the age of thirty.
—*The third* was to have by God's grace three in-depth experiences.

As to the first, I believed that I already had some feeling for the passion of Christ, but I desired yet more, by the grace of God. I thought I would like to have been with Mary Magdalene and with others who were Christ's lovers.

And for this reason I desired to have a bodily sight wherein I might have some knowledge

—of the physical pains of our Savior;
—and of the *compassion*
   —of our Lady
   —and of all his true lovers that at that time saw his pain.

For I wanted to be one of them and to suffer with him. . . .

The reason for this petition was so that after the Showing I would have a truer understanding of the passion of Christ. *The second petition* came to my mind along with *contrition*, whereby I freely desired to have a sickness so serious that I might receive all the rites of Holy Church, thinking that I was going to die; and that all others would believe the same.

For I did not want to find my comfort in this earthly life.

In this sickness I desired to have all the bodily and spiritual pains that I should have if I really died:

—with the fears and temptations coming from the fiend
—all except the passing away of the soul.

I intended this:

—so that I would undergo purgation by the mercy of God and after that live more perfectly in the worship of God because of that sickness.
—And also to hasten my actual death, for I desired to be speedily with God.

These two desires concerning the passion and the sickness I desired conditionally, saying: "Lord you know what it is I desire, if it accords with your will. And if it is not your will, good Lord, be not displeased.

—For I desire nothing but what you will."

As to the third, by the grace of God and the teaching of Holy Church, I formed in my mind a powerful desire to receive three depth experiences in my spirit: that is to say,

—the experience of kind *compassion*;
—the experience of true *contrition*;
—and the experience of a deliberate *longing for God.*

And all of this last petition I asked for without any conditions.

COMMENTARY

Except for the third petition, this prayer might seem rash and foolish. It bears the marks of Julian's youth and of some of the devotional currents of her time. But the prayer is still right, not because, objectively, Julian had asked for the right thing; she is uncertain about this herself.

Its rightness consists in her asking with a right mind and heart: for purposes related to her salvation, and in partnership with the purposes of God. Or, as she says in her short text, prayer must be in accord with the will of God.

Above all, the prayer is grounded in trust: We do not have to tell God what to do, or mistrust what God wants for us.

Julian's conditional desires proceed from a faith which knows that some things are indeed in the will of God: that we should have contrition (regarding ourselves); compassion (for ourselves, others, and the suffering Christ); and that we should summon the power of our will and intention to long for God.

God was the ground of this prayer—though when it was fulfilled it seemed to be merely a natural event in the course of life. But Julian had prepared herself with the proper dispositions of mind and heart, so that her near-death experience became the foundation for one of the most wonderful gifts God has given to her and to the church of God.

At the Approach of Death

I thought that all the time that I had lived here was so little and so short in comparison to the bliss of heaven: I thought that the time I had lived was as nothing.

And so I thought: "Good Lord, can it be that my living on is no longer to your honor?" And I understood through my reason and by the feeling of my pains that I should die.

I assented fully to everything, with all the strength of my heart, to be at God's will.

Chapter 3

COMMENTARY

This prayer is especially fitting for the dying. It will spring spontaneously to the lips if we have previously crushed the illusion that we are somehow immortal; and that death is something that happens only to others. Julian longs for the happiness of heaven—a fulfillment to which the whole of life bears no comparison.

But dying remains a mystery. One writer's reflections on this capture the mix of fulfillment and emptiness that death seems to hold:

> The imminence of death . . . becomes the greatest challenge to the true obedience that is required of us throughout life: doing what it is given to us to do—in this case returning life itself to the Creator and falling without security into divine hands. If we can believe this, we can indeed hope to be responsible and free people with respect to our deaths. For at death we need a final obedience that actively summarizes the obedient responsibility of our whole lives.[1]

It may be easy to trivialize the notion of the will of God, applying it to events which, in fact, we cause ourselves. But we cannot trivialize the destiny of death. Every acceptance of emptiness, every act of letting go of what has seemed a precious part of our lives, prepares for this final effort to do what is given us to do. Julian models for us how to accept life as a time of responsible action and to long for heaven, too.

What do we make of the fact that Julian's prayer—to die at this moment—is not literally fulfilled? Why was it important for her to pray this way anyhow? These questions are answered in part later in her account of her reflections.

Women mystics have often been portrayed as passive, as simply allowing God—or others—to shape their lives. But Julian illustrates what it means to act responsibly by the way she is ready to die responsibly. Jesus said, "My work is finished," and yielded himself to his Father. Julian asks if her work is finished. If it is, then she reaches out for what she has been tending toward—happiness without end in a transformed and transfigured life.

We might speculate what went through Julian's mind and heart at the time when she actually did die, after the Showings and the years of reflection on them.

O Blessed Lord!

Then suddenly I saw the red blood trickling down from under the garland. . . . as it may have been at the time of the passion. I saw and understood truly and powerfully that God himself showed this to me, *without any intermediary*.

And in the same Showing suddenly the Trinity filled my heart with the greatest *joy*. And so I understood that it shall be in heaven without end, for all that come there . . . for where Jesus is seen, the Trinity is understood, as I see it. And I said: "O blessed Lord!"

Chapter 4

COMMENTARY

Julian's mystical insight is to know that the Trinity is present, though it is Jesus whom she sees.

The sign of that presence is joy—overwhelming joy.

The sight and the presence come suddenly. She does not at the moment even make any connection between what she saw and her youthful prayer to be a loving witness to the passion. The suddenness of these graces indicates that they may be from God, though later she will doubt that this is so.

Some teachers of prayer trace a path from imaging to silence, which is considered to be the highest experience.

At this point at least Julian does not follow such a path. She looks at the face of Jesus, the head crowned with thorns, and knows that the Trinity is there. She does not keep silence. She speaks out, or at least forms interior words. She is unable to contain her joy, which overflows into her whole being.

If she had been in good health, would she also have broken into dance?

In You I Have All

He showed me a little thing, the size of a hazelnut, in the palm of my hand. . . .

I looked on it with the eye of my understanding and thought: "What can this be?" And it was answered in a general way thus: "It is all that has been made."

I marvelled how it could last. . . . And I was answered in my understanding:

"It lasts, and will last forever because God loves it; and so all things have being by the love of God. . . ." Our Lord God showed that it is very pleasing to him to have a simple soul come to him,

—simply, openly, and intimately.

For, by the prompting of the Holy Ghost, this is what we naturally long for, according to what I understood in this Showing:

"God, of your *goodness*, give me yourself.

—For you are sufficient for me; and I can ask for nothing less and still offer complete worship to you. And if I do ask for anything less, I am left unsatisfied.

—For in You alone I have all."

These words please the soul very much.

And closely touch God's will and God's *goodness*.

"For your *goodness* is found in all your creatures and in all your blessed works, endlessly surpassing them

—for you are the everlasting.

You have *made us* only for yourself; and *restored us* by your blessed passion; and you *keep us* in your blessed love. And all of this is of your *goodness*."

Creator

Carer.

Redeemer

Chapter 5

COMMENTARY

Julian here introduces two important teachings about prayer.

First, praying comes from a natural desire, activated by the Holy Spirit. We are like winged birds in the nest, needing the prompting of the mother bird to do what is natural to us.

Second, prayer arises from a desire for the good, and the good is what we truly desire. Not only do we desire the good, but we are less than content until we have the source of goodness, the very God.

We know this goodness in the creatures God has made.

But God's goodness surpasses that of all creatures, as the source surpasses what flows from it. God endures forever. Does the creator share this endlessness with creatures? The vision of the hazelnut suggests this, since the mystery of it is that it lasts. It lasts, of course, by being transformed.

This goodness to which we are drawn is the living Trinity.

> —There is the person *who made us* full of these great desires;
> —There is the Christ *who restored us* (the only intimation at this point of sin);
> —There is the Holy Spirit, acting in us, *caring for us* through love.

What Julian saw in the hazelnut, she now sees in her own yearnings: the maker, the lover, the keeper.

These three signs of the goodness of God are acclaimed and intertwined in verses from the Book of Wisdom:

The maker:
> For you love all things that are
> and loathe nothing that you have made;
> for what you despised you would not have fashioned.

The keeper:
> And how could a thing remain, unless you willed it;
> or be preserved, had it not been called forth by you?

The lover:
> But you spare all things, because they are yours, O LORD
> and lover of souls (Wis. 11:24–26).

Pray first to have the very God—all goodness. Let us try to use Julian's short prayer—at least in its intent. "It is you yourself I long for, O God. All else is less and will not bring me rest."

We are to come before God just as we are, not frightened off by our limitations.

Is this not in the pattern of the Our Father, "Lord's Prayer" which begins with beholding God's happiness (heaven) and with proclaiming the holiness of the divine name?

The Focus
of Prayer:

The Goodness
of God

By What Means Should We Approach God?

At that time there came to my mind the customs of our ways
of praying and how
—for lack of *understanding*
—and lack of *knowledge of love*
we use many "means."
Then I saw in truth that it is more to the glory of God, and
more delightful, for us to pray faithfully directly to God as
goodness.
And cling thereto by grace,
—with true *understanding*
—and by steadfast *love*.
This is better than if we used all the "means" that our hearts
could devise. For if we do use these "means,"
—it is all too little and not fully to the glory of God.
But in God's *goodness* there is everything;
And there is nothing lacking.
And there came to my mind at the same time how we pray to
God through his holy flesh, his precious blood, his holy passion, his dearworthy death and wounds:
—but all the blessed kindness and endless life that
comes to us from all these is *of his goodness*.
And again, we pray to him by the love of the sweet mother
who bore him:
—but all the help we have through her is *of his goodness*.
And we pray by that holy cross on which he died:
—but all the virtue and help that we have from the cross is
of his goodness.
Likewise, in just the same way, all the help we have of special
saints and of all the blessed company of heavens:
—the precious love and endless friendship that we have of
them: it is all *of his goodness*.
But God *of his goodness* has ordained "means" to help us—all
fair and plenteous. The chief and principal means is the
blessed nature that he took of the maid

—with all the "means" that went before and come after which belong to our redemption and to our eternal salvation.

It pleases him, then, that we seek him and give glory to him by "means"

—*understanding* and *knowing* that God is *the goodness* of all.

Chapter 6

COMMENTARY

Julian, on first reading, seems to contradict herself on this subject of using means to approach God. But is this so?

In the first part she echoes what she has already taught: that we may stand before God in all simplicity (Chapter 5). She stresses that God is so open to us, so unconditionally good, that we do not need to make an indirect approach. We do not need to call on Mary or the other saints to plead our cause, or to make our petitions acceptable to God, as though God were deaf to us.

What seems at first most startling is that we do not even have to approach God through the mediation of Christ and his crucifixion. What Julian means here, of course, is that these actions of Christ did not change God from wrath to compassion. God never ceased to love us; rather, the passion revealed God's love for us most fully.

Contemporaries of Julian, such as the the author of *The Cloud of Unknowing* and mystics in the Lowlands, urged their disciples to seek to know God, or to love God, "without intermediary." From God's side, Julian teaches, there is a sound basis for such a practice—so long as it is to the goodness of God that we address ourselves. But Julian is not speaking to such specialized practitioners of perfect prayer. She is speaking to her even-Christians. They may have been wrongly taught that, because of their unworthiness, they should seek a go-between for speaking to God. Or they themselves may feel that they should ask for extra help because their own petitions are not apt to carry much weight with a majestic God.

We do not need means. God is accessible to all of us because God is goodness.

All we need is true understanding and steadfast love.

So why, then, does Julian seem to make an about-face in the middle of the passage? "God out of goodness has ordained means to help us"?

The "means" are just that: to help *us*, not to manipulate or persuade or get a favorable hearing from God. Those who pray for us are often more practiced in being open to God.

Then Julian lists again those customary components of our prayer. These begin with the Christ born of Mary. They include all that was revealed in the Hebrew Scriptures and all that will come later under the guidance of the Holy Spirit. Among these are the help we find in particular saints; and with those of our own departed with whom we retain ties of precious love and endless friendship.

So, do we need "means" in our approach to God? Not if this implies that we doubt God's goodness. But yes, inasmuch as we need what we can see and experience in order to know and love God rightfully. We are in solidarity with our holy friends, who pray with us and for us. We speak to God of them, too, affirming our love and joining our petitions and praise to theirs.

God's Goodness Encircles the Whole

For the *goodness* of God is the highest prayer
    And it comes down to the lowliest part of our need.
    It quickens the soul and brings it to birth;
    And makes it grow in grace and virtue.
It is nearest to us in nature, and promptest to us in grace.
    —That is the same grace which the soul seeks, and ever
        shall, until we know truly the one in whom we are en-
        closed.
For God does not look down on anything that is made.
And God does not disdain to serve us in the simplest office
that belongs to our body by nature, for love of the soul that is
made to the divine likeness. . . . .
For truly our lover desires that we cling to him with our
whole soul, with all our strength;
and that we forever hold fast to God's *goodness* . . . .
our soul is particularly loved by the one who is highest, with
a love that surpasses anything that creatures could know. . . .
And therefore, with God's grace and help,
    we may stand
    —*beholding* our God spiritually, marvelling without end
        —at this high, inconceivable, all-surpassing love al-
        mighty God has for us *out of goodness.*
And therefore we may reverently *ask* of our Lover whatever
we will:
    —for by nature we incline to have God and God's desire is
        to have us.
    And we can never cease wanting nor longing till we have
God in fullness of joy;
    —and then we can no longer want for anything.
But *God* wills that we keep occupied in
    —*knowing*
    —and *loving*
Until that time when we shall be fulfilled in heaven. . . .
The *beholding* and the *loving* of the maker cause us to see our-

selves as least, in our own eyes; and fills us full of *reverent dread* and *true meekness*.

—with abundant charity for our even-Christians.

And to teach us this, as to my understanding, our Lord God showed Our Lady, saint Mary, at the same time: that is, there was shown the high wisdom and truth she had in the *beholding* of her maker—so high, mighty, and good. The greatness and the dignity of the beholding of God filled her

—with *reverent dread*;

And with this, she saw herself so little and so low, so simple and so poor, in relation to the Lord God,

— that this *reverent dread* filled her with *meekness*.

And thus, on this ground,

—she was fulfilled in grace;

—and in all manner of virtues;

—and surpasses all other creatures.

Chapters 6 and 7

COMMENTARY

Sophia

These passages suggest what is developed explicitly in later chapters: the one whom we behold in prayer is our Mother Christ, Word and Wisdom, God and man.

We are conceived in the womb of Christ, given birth in him, and our growth is fostered by him. This divine motherhood is goodness.

Since this goodness is in all creation, God loves all that is made. We can, therefore, behold the goodness of God as we live by and with the goodness of creation. The self-centered ego shrinks away under the act of drinking in, with our eyes, the goodness in the seed, the leaf, the flower, the face of one who is loved, as well as the invisible God. If that goodness returns our meditative gaze, we feel great awe. "For the goodness that all things have—it is God" (Chapter 8).

In times before the Showings, Julian had simply let her senses rest on the multitude of the drops of water in a rain shower—how uncountable those drops, how unfathomable their sound. At other times she had delighted in the patterns of herring scales—how they spread out, one after the other.

She was fully alive to the wonder, mystery, and depths of what she saw, heard, and touched. Such a habit of mind served her when the greater graces of the Showings opened in her consciousness. Beauty and vitality were words she had already filled with meaning, before she saw the bleeding brow of Christ. Particularly, the simple looking toward God overflows into love for her even-Christians. She grows in compassion.

How are we to learn this and the effects of the prayer of simple beholding? In Mary. It is in this way that she becomes a "means" for us: she is a supereminent reflection of the goodness of Mother Christ, by beholding—"pondering," as the Scripture says—the creator who encloses us all. At this point Mary learns motherhood from God the Mother, and later Christ Incarnate learned the human dimension of motherhood from her.

Blessed Be God!

[As] long as I saw the sight of the plenteous bleeding of the head, I could never stop saying these words: "O, blessed be God!"

In *seeing* this showing I also *understood* these things:

—that the blessed Godhead was, is, and ever shall be;

—that God made all things out of love;

—and by that same love all things are now preserved and will be without end.

—that God is everything that is good, as I see it;

—and that the goodness that all things have—it is God. . . .

And in all this *I was deeply moved with love for my even-Christians*

—that they might *see* and *know* the same as I saw;

—for I wanted it to be a comfort to them. . . .

What I say of myself I say in the person of my even-Christians; for I was taught in the spiritual showing of our Lord God that is how it is meant. Therefore, I beg you, for God's sake, and counsel you, for your own profit, that you leave off *beholding* the poor creature it was shown to and mightily, *wisely,* and meekly *behold* God who in *courteous* love and endless *goodness* wishes to show it generally for the comfort of us all.

It is God's will that you take it *with great joy and delight,* as though Jesus had shown it to one and all.

Chapter 8

COMMENTARY

Julian's way of praying is to see, and to know what is meant by what she sees.

For us this may mean picturing in our minds what we are already familiar with: the face of Christ in his passion. The face does not need to be visually explicit. It is rather the way we call up in memory the visage of absent or deceased friends, perhaps holding in our hand a photograph of them.

This act makes us feel that we are somehow again in their presence. We know perhaps better than before the meaning of their lives and what lies behind their surface likeness.

What is important in this act of seeing or picturing is to understand what the face of Christ means. Julian lists what she knows through faith—truths that are burned into her consciousness—by connecting them with the crowned head of Christ. So deep is this awareness that words spring to her lips—or are formed in her heart—as an overflow of what she sees and understands.

Never does Julian see herself as in a position of privilege, nor does she consider her conversing with Christ as special to herself. She feels love for her even-Christians in the midst of her prayer, desiring intensely that they, too, see and know as she does. Later she will realize that she has a role in helping them to share her experiences.

Julian's prayer reaches across the ages to us, too. She has immense charity for us. We have her for a friend. Her writings teach us to understand prayer.

We observe that Julian does not have a system, in the sense that we take one step after another in order to pray. While praying with her, we do everything all at once: we see and visualize Christ; we realize that God is actively present in all creation; and that God acts in love and through love. We call up a memory, full of meaning and promise. We may even form words to exclaim over what we are taking in, the way we do at times when confronted with immense beauty—of the mountains or the sea. We do all this in solidarity of spirit with others.

Julian's special gift is to be able to hold in her awareness all at once that God is in Christ, and Christ is in God, and that God is also in us as collective humanity.

Not for the Wise

I am not good because of the Showing, but only if I love God the better. . . .I do not say this for those who are *wise,* for they know it well. But I say it to you who are simple, for your ease and comfort

——for we are all one in comfort. . . .

I am sure that there are many who never had showing or sight——except of the common teaching of holy church——who love God better than I.

For if I look to myself alone, I am really nothing; but if I look at myself in the whole body, I am in hope——seeing myself in oneness of charity with all my even-Christians. . .

God is all that is good, as I see it,

and God has made all that is made;

and God loves all that is made;

And we who love all our even-Christians for God,

we love all that is;

For in humankind that shall be saved is included all that is. . .

In our humanity is God, and God is in all.

I hope by the grace of God that the ones who behold it thus shall be truly taught and greatly comforted, if they need comfort.

Chapter 9

COMMENTARY

Where should we look for God when we pray? Not in visions or unusual happenings.

The vision of God conveyed to us in the common teaching of the church is enough for us. We do not pray relying on our own strength but taking comfort in that invisible union which makes us one with all believers. In that union we all together make up the body of Christ: we are one with him as the branches are one with the vine. The vine is in the branches, and the branches are in the vine, though the vine is the whole and the branches are the parts. The same life runs through all.

This is a great mystery and easily misunderstood. Julian guides us to pray with the mystery of the Incarnation before us. We can pause before prayer and ask that all the saints in heaven join us. We can further feel solace in knowing that others pray as we do and that we love and hope in God by the same Spirit. We can actually join in prayer with some of those believers, who represent the multitudes who hope in God.

The "wise"—those who are learned in theology and human psychology—know that love, not visions, matters. Do these "wise" also know in a practical way that all believers—"even-Christians"—are one in Christ and hence equal in God's way of seeing? Both the simple and the wise need to be taught how this lesson applies to prayer.

Julian guides us into becoming wise about prayer by leading us into deeper understanding and more faithful love.

The Prayer of Desire

And after this I saw with bodily sight on the face of the crucifix . . . a part of the passion . . . and I *desired more* bodily sight so as to see more clearly.

And I was answered in my reason: "If God will show you more, God will be your light. You need none but God."

For I *saw* you and I *sought* you.

We are now so blind and foolish that we never seek you until out of your *goodness* you show yourself to us.

And if we *see* something of you by grace, then we are moved by the same grace to *seek* with great *desire* to *see* you in even greater bliss.

And thus I *saw* you and I *sought* you;

And I had you and still *desired* you.

This is, and should be, our ordinary working in this, as I see it.
. . .

And this vision was a lesson to my understanding

that the soul's continual *seeking* pleases God very much.

For the soul can do no more than *seek*, suffer, and trust;

And this is accomplished in the soul that has it by the Holy Ghost.

And the clearness of *finding* is a special grace when it is God's will.

The *seeking*, with faith, hope, and charity, pleases our Lord; and the *finding* pleases the soul and fills it with *joy*.

And thus was I taught in my understanding

—that *seeking* is as good as *beholding*

—during the time that God allows us to be in travail.

It is your will that we *seek* you until we *behold* you,

—for you will show yourself by a special grace when you so will.

And how a soul shall possess you in this *beholding* you yourself shall teach.

That is most to the glory of God and of most profit to us

and makes us most to receive meekness and virtues
—through the *leading* of the Holy Ghost.
For those who cling to God
—with true *trust*
—either in *seeking*
—or in *beholding*
Give the most glory to God—as far as it can be—as I see it,
These are two workings that are seen in this vision:
—the one is *seeking;*
—the other is *beholding.*
The *seeking* is common—everyone may *seek* by God's grace
And ought to, with the discernment and teaching of holy
church.
It is God's will that we have three things in our *seeking*:
—the *first* is that we *seek* God intently and purposefully
—without *sloth,* as well as we can with God's grace,
gladly and merrily without unreasonable heaviness and
vain sorrow.
—the *second* is that we *await* God steadfastly, knowing we
are loved,
—without grumbling and resisting grace, to the end of
our life, for it shall last but a while.
—the *third* is that we *trust* mightily with complete
faith, for this is God's will.
We know you will appear suddenly and joyfully to all your
lovers.
For your working is in secret
—yet you will to be perceived.
Your appearing will be most sudden
—and you will be believed.
For God is both courteous and common, awesome and ordinary.
Blessed be God!

Chapter 10

COMMENTARY
Julian lays down a preliminary principle here that, in her case
and in ours, the first prompting in prayer comes from God.

She also explains what we are to do and what we may expect. The experience of the second Showing—of the face of Christ seen dimly—is a short parable about prayer. Christ shows his suffering face. She wants to see more. She realizes that she must wait until the light which is God unveils more of that divine face and its mysteries. While waiting she does not allow her desire to wane.

From this experience she draws out a lesson for our ordinary way of praying. God breaks through our blindness with an insight or good desire. We know it is God's working. Stirring up our own desires we seek assurance that God will give more.

Then we are at a standstill, even beset by doubt. What good is this emptiness, made all the more painful after temporary peace?

Then another law of praying: To seek God is as good as to know we have God. This is how it is most of the time. We learn that we do not get control of God, that we cannot predict God's ways, that we cannot answer the "why" that trouble raises in us.

Some lines from Jessica Powers describe this time of waiting:

God sits on a chair of darkness in my soul. . .
I sit at his feet, a child in the dark beside Him.[1]

Only in God's time will the beholding come. It is often as surprising as a thunderbolt, and not in the time and place of prayer at all. God's timing often strikes us as absurd: "I was having trouble with this old washing machine and saying my customary prayer—'Christ, be before me'—when suddenly...." "I was on my way to visit detainees in the prison, when it came to me in a flash. . . ."

"I was recovering in the hospital, wondering in my pain: 'Where, really, is Christ?' when I looked up and knew that Christ was in the hands offering me my tray."

In such language the ordinary person hesitantly describes the suddenness of God's visitation in the midst of daily life.

The suddenness is a mark of God's visitation. It also serves to remind us that, though God wants us to seek, it is not the method or power of our seeking that brings the divine presence into our lives. We do not tear away the veil of darkness over God's face. Seeking gives way to beholding—as God wills.

God teaches us also how to make the effects of this beholding last. Powers has something to say, too, about "clinging to God." The garment of God is rough and coarse—the stuff of life and daily living. (God is awesome and yet approachable.)

> He is clothed in the robes of His mercy, voluminous garments . . . .
> Not velvet or silk or affable to the touch,
> but fabric strong for a frantic hand to clutch,
> and hold it fast with the fingers of my will. . . .
> here in the dark I clutch the garments of my God.

Having expanded her parable and drawn some lessons from it, Julian adds a clear summary about (a) God's action, and (b) ours.

God works in us to seek and to behold—"to desire and to accomplish."

We work in partnership with God, in seeking, according to this simple program: seek diligently, wait merrily, and trust mightily.

1. We seek God with serious intent but with a merry heart—a hallmark of Julian's plan for living. With enthusiasm, to counter sloth, which leads to dragging our feet, bemoaning our state, and taking perverse comfort in the darkness rather than the light.

2. This merry heart shows itself in patient waiting for God. Even if we wait our entire lives, that is not very long. We remember that the first Christians expected the second coming within their own lifetime. But it was not to be. They waited, however, in acts of remembrance and in the singing of songs and hymns.

3. Merrily we wait, in trust. We live with ambiguity, not even knowing if our choices are objectively right. We trust, when the stones of our earthly security crumble into shapeless sand.

Then there is a divine program, too:

God works "graciously"—by grace, helping us; with grace, revealing a loving countenance.

God works, too, in the very texture of life as it is, in what is most familiar to us, in homely ways. (God is holy and homely).

Julian did not worry about how one God could be three persons, or such mysteries. What she found amazing was that God is both gracious and homely, noble and near, awesome and approachable. . . .

"Holy and homely God: You are blessed in all your ways." Julian gazes at God in the half-darkness and is loud with praise.

God in a Point

11. [In the third vision] I saw God in a point . . .
   —by which sight I saw that God is in all things. . . .
And I saw truly that nothing is done by accident or chance,
but everything by the foreseeing *wisdom* of God. . . .
And this vision was shown *to my understanding,* because our
Lord God would have the soul turned truly to the beholding
of the one who is,
   —generally
   —and in all God's works.
For they are full good;
And all that God does is easy and sweet;
   —and puts greatly at ease the soul that is turned from beholding blindly, as creatures judge, to beholding fairly and
   sweetly, as our Lord God judges. . . .
For as all that has being in nature is of God's *making,*
so likewise, everything that is done, is in virtue of God's *doing. . . .*
And all this was shown full blissfully, meaning thus:
   —"See, I am God.
   —"See, I am in all things.
   —"See, I do all things.
   —"See, I never lift my hands from my work, nor never
   shall, without end."

Chapter 11

COMMENTARY
Not all share in Julian's experience of seeing God in a point—
that is, as permeating and active in all things.[2]

   But she leads all of us, through a simple image and through
reason and reflection, to profit from what she saw.

   The image is of God's hands—crafting, comforting, and directing all things to a good end.

   We know about hands and how mysteriously they transmit
human intelligence, power, and purpose to what they mold

and shape. God's hands make manifest the power, wisdom, and love which pour out from the Trinity. They are the Trinity.

Earlier teachers, such as St. Ambrose, used the metaphor of God's hands to signify oneness of power in the Trinity.

The Father creates us. "Your hands have made me and fashioned me" (Ps. 119:73). "My hand made all these things" (Is. 66:2).

Mother Christ cradles us. "Can a mother forget her infant? . . . See, upon the palms of my hands/ I have written your name" (Is. 49:15–16).

The Spirit comforts us: "For the LORD comforts his people/and shows mercy to his afflicted" (Is. 49:13).

St. Ireneus (d. 208) "described the Son and the Spirit as being the two hands of the Father, touching us and moulding us to his image and likeness."[3]

Julian's hands were often busied with lace work and weaving, where it is important to keep a steady touch lest the whole be marred.

God's hands make all things good.

Calling on our understanding, we must conclude that all that is done is well done.

But of course we see what look like evil deeds, and so did Julian.

She is not going to deny sin or turn her eyes away from evil. But that reflection is for later. Now we try to enter into how God sees and judges.

She invites us to rest in the truth she sees so compellingly— the goodness of all creation, even the least deed.

We do not set aside our reason and understanding here. Rather, we assimilate one truth at a time and prepare to wrestle later with how it integrates with other parts of experience, often more compelling than belief in goodness.

Can we assent to this? If so, we shall share in Julian's moment of joy. "I will hear what God proclaims" (Ps. 85:9).

Christ
the Center
of Prayer

(nothing from it)

Prayer of Listening

And afterwards, before God showed any words, I was per-
mitted for an appropriate time to *behold* in him
   —all that I had *seen*
   —and all that I had *understood*
as the simplicity of the soul could take it in.
Then, without voice or opening of lips, God forms in my soul
these words:
   "Herewith is the fiend overcome."
By these words he meant his blessed passion, as he had
shown it to me before.
In this our Lord showed that in his passion is the overcoming
of the fiend. . . .
The power of the fiend is all held in God's hand. . . .
On judgment day the fiend shall see that all the woe and tribulation that he has caused to those who shall be saved will in-
crease their joy without end;
And all the pain and tribulation that he brought on them shall
go eternally with him into hell.

Chapter 13

COMMENTARY

Julian prays here by simply resting in what she has seen of the
passion and how she has reasoned about its efficacy. What
has gone before now seeps into her soul effortlessly. She is not
raising the question of sin or evil.

This is the prayer of listening.

For some the practice of prayer consists in turning away
from thoughts or impressions in prayer—even holy ones—in
order to rest only in God.

At this moment, this is not Julian's way.

She accepts what she hears in her heart: *"The power of the
fiend is all held in God's hand."* Again, God's hand stands for
God's power, this time conserving the good creation.

John's Gospel (10:28–30) reports such words from Christ's

teaching. Christ protects us from the thief and the intruder.

Of those who hear his voice he says:

I give them eternal life and they shall never perish. No one can take them out of my hand. My Father, who has given them to me is greater than all and no one can take them out of the Father's hand. The Father and I are one.

This time Julian does not end with any words. Sometimes they seem unneeded.

It is the time for silence.

Faith Without Feeling

I had no comfort nor no ease, but only faith, hope, and charity.

These I had in fact;
but little in feeling. . . .
After this, our blessed Lord gave me again comfort and rest of soul.

And then I felt the *pain* come again;
And then the *joy* and the *delight*;
And now the one, and then the other, many times.
In the time of *joy*,
I might have said with Saint Paul: "Nothing shall separate me from the charity of Christ."
And in the *pain*, I might have said with Peter: "Lord, save me, I perish" . . .
It is God's will

—that we keep ourselves in *comfort* with all our strength
—for *bliss* is *lasting* and without end;
—and *pain* is *passing* and will be brought to nothing for those who shall be saved.

And it *is not* God's will

—that we hold on to those feelings of *pain*, sorrowing, and mourning because of them;
—but we should quickly pass them by and keep ourselves in unending *enjoying*.

Chapter 15

COMMENTARY

The plan of this little teaching on prayer is a familiar one:

—First, Julian tells the story of her struggles.
—Then, she tells us how she might pray during these times
—And finally, she explains to us, clearly and directly,
—what dispositions we should counter and which ones foster, in pain or in joy.

Sometimes spiritual guidebooks try to tell us that in prayer feelings do not matter. Julian does not say this.

She is more realistic.

True, faith is more important than feelings.

But the point of Julian's instruction is

—first, how to use our feelings as a powerful incentive to
prayer.

> —Notice she says, I might have prayed thus and so. She
> does not prescribe these expressions for all.

> —She leaves it open to us to prepare in advance for
> times when feelings surge so powerfully that we are in
> no state to search for appropriate ways to pray.

—Second, how to *see* our feelings in their relative value:

> —pain is passing

> —joy is forever.

We need to find a prayer to express this, too. Not a saying
from the philosophers but a prayer.

A prayer of the Psalmist may perhaps serve:

> "For you make me jubilant, O LORD, by your deeds;

> > at the works of your hands I shout for joy" (Ps. 92:5).

It is a prayer that has its roots in faith.

The Cross Is the Way

Then I heard a suggestion coming from my reason, as if from a friendly voice, which said: "Look up to heaven to his Father...." I either had to look up, or to give an answer.
I answered, inwardly, with all the power of my soul and said:
"No, I cannot. For you are my heaven...."
Thus I was taught to choose only Jesus for my heaven, though I saw him only in pain at that time....
This was a lesson to me that I should evermore
—choose only Jesus for my heaven
—in weal
—and in woe.
And though like a wretch I regretted having made my request [to suffer with Christ] (... For if I had known what pain it would be to me, I would have been loath to have prayed thus) Here I saw truly that this regret came from
—the flesh
—complaining
—and condemning
—without assent from the soul.
To this God assigns no blame.

Chapter 19

COMMENTARY
What could be wrong with "looking up to heaven" in time of pain?
Julian's reason tries to mislead her.
Our reason may at times delude us into thinking of prayer as a substitute for facing the reality of human suffering. Sometimes we hear this in the form of advice to the under-privileged: to endure their impoverished condition stoically, for the world of the spirit is all that matters.
Sometimes prayer is offered to us as an escape from the suffering going on around us.
The saints are often pictured as living on Earth in an aura of bliss.

But in choosing Jesus for her heaven, Julian embraces the reality of human suffering, which, united to the suffering Christ, can be transformed into joy.

How hard she finds it to hold fast to the choice she has made: to join her experience of dying with that of Christ dying, in the presence of others who suffered with him.

In refusing to "look up to heaven," she acknowledges that God is entangled in the reality of the world in which we live.

Just as she does not use prayer as an escape from the reality of the suffering of Christ and his members, so, likewise, she does not sink down into self-blame for her faltering resolution.

She does not picture God as adding to her suffering with a burden of guilt for her weakness.

Julian's heaven is not a disembodied dream. It is the deep happiness of compassion, of the love made known to us when Christ was hanging, rejected, on the cross.

If we can learn to discern it, this will give meaning to our lives.

It is not something remote from our lives, but meets us in every human situation, wherever people suffer and are oppressed, wherever people are imprisoned, tortured and killed, wherever people are dying of cancer or of AIDS, wherever drink and drugs and crime are destroying people's lives. There, *if we can learn to discern it,* this mystery of love is present. It is the reality which gives meaning to human existence which challenges us in every situation of life. That reality . . . was revealed in its fullness when Jesus was hanging on the cross, rejected, despised, humiliated, exposed to hatred and violence, to pain and death. It was then that the true nature of reality was made known, the truth for which science and philosophy are seeking, which holds the answer to the paradox of existence. It was then that love itself was revealed, it is that which gives ultimate meaning to our lives.[1]

JULIAN: The Eighth Showing

The Risen Christ Is With Us in Our Pain

As long as Christ could suffer
  —he did suffer and he sorrowed *for* us.
  And now that he is risen and can suffer no more
  —he suffers *with* us.
Beholding all this by grace, I saw that the love which Christ has
for our soul is so strong that he willingly chose what he suffered, and he suffered it patiently at great cost.
  For the soul that *beholds* it thus, when touched by grace,
  will truly see that the pains of Christ *surpass* all pains—that
  is to say
  —those pains will be turned into eternal, *surpassing joys*
    —by virtue of Christ's passion.

Chapter 20

COMMENTARY

Julian's prayer of beholding is an attentive gaze of the understanding, aroused to a state of wonder, and overflowing into
the feelings.

The mystery she beholds here is that time and eternity are
interwoven, for Christ and for us.

This is a great mystery, to be wondered at in faith and
thanks.

Julian when contemplating the dying of Christ saw no time
elapse between the death and the new life: the face of Christ
sorrowing was in an instant the face of Christ glorified.

It is not enough to say that time and its sufferings do not
matter.

They do matter. They are the groundwork of eternal joy.
They give the shape and character to the kind of heaven we
will have.

Julian wants us to behold a great truth: Christ suffers and
rises in us. Christ suffered and rose—yes—but it is happening
now, not in a sequence of events such as we picture the passage of time. The life of the risen Christ, as well as of the suffering Christ, is at work in us now.

She beheld this truth by grace, observing that Christ suffered willingly and patiently.

She says if we look on Christ rightly, we too will experience the mystery of the suffering-risen Christ in our lives.

Julian lived in and through the dying of Christ because that was the event she seemed to be experiencing in her severe illness.

We can copy her way by finding a sorrow in Christ's life that is like the one we are undergoing. It will be like two friends who endure together a pain of loss or other form of suffering. The pain of the one is shared by the other and, in a sense, increases the pain, but in a transcending, surpassing way—so that one suffers in community with others, not in isolation and inward turning. The suffering together is the growing place for love.

"Lo, How I Love You"

With this sweet *beholding*
   —He showed his blessed heart, cut in two.
And with this sweet *rejoicing*
   —He showed to my understanding
      —in part, the blessed Godhead
Stirring the pure soul to understand . . .
   —the endless love, that was without beginning,
   and is, and shall be forever.
And with this our good Lord said most blissfully:
"Lo, how I have loved you."

Chapter 24

COMMENTARY

Julian told us at the beginning that where Jesus is, there is the Trinity.

Here she works this out in a particular way.

She pictures the heart of Christ, pierced because his love led him to the passion.

Then, stirred by grace, she becomes aware that this love manifests the Trinity.

   —As before, the sign of the presence of the Trinity is joy. ←

She rejoices. How easy it would be to take this overwhelming assurance of love as an occasion of feelings of guilt—since we respond so inadequately. But Christ's purpose is to make us merry.

Christ's assurance of love is, as Julian told us, too, at the beginning, not to be taken by herself alone.

Nor just transferred to us individually either.

It is God's word of love to all who come to him.

How can we doubt it?

This Is Said to Make Us Merry

"How should it now be that you should pray for anything that pleases me, without my gladly granting it to you?

"For my good pleasure is your holiness, and your endless joy is bliss with me."

This is the understanding [I had], as simply as I can say it, of the blessed word: "Lo, how I loved you."

Our Lord showed this to make us glad and merry.

Chapter 24

COMMENTARY

We often ask ourselves the wrong questions about prayer.

We want to pray for "what pleases God." But how do we do that?

The answer to that query is hard to take in: God is pleased by whatever is for our best interests—whatever will help make us holy and bring lasting joy.

We can understand this in part, for it is just what we want for those we truly love.

How gracious of God to let us know this now and not leave us wondering what formulas or offerings might appease a mysterious and distant Deity.

God lets us know this simple truth to make us "glad and merry."

It follows, then, that being "glad and merry" in the real sense is a means to holiness.

We cannot, of course, be "glad and merry" alone. God wants "us" to be glad and merry—to be happy together in the warm light of faith.

Especially after we have prayed together.

"But I Did Not See Her"

Our good Lord . . . brought to my mind where our Lady stood
at the time of his passion and said:
  "Do you want to see her?. . ."
  "Do you want to see how I love her?. . ."
  "Would you like to see in her how you are loved?"
Herein I am not taught
  —to long to see her bodily presence while I am here;
  —but to see the virtues of her soul
    —her truth, her wisdom, her charity.
Whereby I may learn
  —to know myself
  —and reverently to stand in awe of my God.
And when our good Lord had shown this and said this word:
  "Do you want to see her?"
I answered and said: "Yes, good Lord, please. Yes, good Lord,
if it be your will."
I often prayed thus, and I wanted to see her in bodily pres-
ence.
But I saw her not so.

Chapter 26

COMMENTARY

Julian is utterly one of us here, where she prays persistently
for what she finally learns is not of use to her.

Christians through the ages have longed to see Mary with
bodily eyes. Julian was among them.

What Christ wanted her to learn was best understood by
focusing on what Mary was, not on what she looked like, nor
how she was dressed. To see Mary in her individuality might
distract from the teaching that she stands for all of us: women
and men and the corporate reality which is the church, especially as it will be in heaven. Nor is it said here that Mary is
a woman who repaired what another woman, Eve, brought
about. Mary is that humanity which is greatly loved.

To see Mary as she actually was at the foot of the cross could distract from the kind of existence we will all have after the body has died. Mary is all of us come to fulfillment.

Note that Julian says: "I was *not* taught" to ask to see her. She found out that such was not God's will only by experience.

She listened faithfully to God, but she did not at once fully understand what God meant by "seeing" Mary.

Because her prayer was not granted in the way Julian desired, she learned more about herself and learned better how to "fear"—to stand in awe of God. Phrases from the Magnificat—the prayer attributed to Mary in Luke's Gospel—took deeper root in her memory: "[God's] mercy is from age to age/to those who fear him" (Lk. 1:50).[2]

Seeing Julian on the wrong track here illustrates what we learned from her earlier: we pray as best we can.

We may not always be praying "for the right thing." But we can always be praying "with a right heart."

We have learned from Julian's experience. Therefore we can pray to see in Mary how we are loved.

"I Am All That Is"

After this. . . I was taught that our soul will never be at rest until we come to God, knowing that
   —God is the fullness of joy
   —God is blessed—and both homely and courteous
   —God is true life.
Our Lord Jesus oftentimes said:
"It is I . . .
"It is I . . .
"I am the one who is."
"It is I who am the highest.
   "It is I whom you love."
   "It is I in whom you delight."
   "It is I for whom you long."
   "It is I whom you desire."
   "It is I whom you serve."
   "It is I whom you intend."
"I am all that is."
"It is I whom holy church teaches and preaches to you.
"It is I who showed myself here to you. . . ."
   The *joy* that I saw in this showing surpasses all that heart may will and soul may desire. . . .
   Let every one, according to the grace that God gives to each of us,
   —in understanding and loving
      —receive these words as God intends them.

                                                              Chapter 26

COMMENTARY
Here we learn, first, how to know that it is God whom we seek. God is made known in true joy, which alone stills the restlessness of our hearts; in that which is holy, whether in familiar ways or awe-inspiring ways; and in that which has true life.
   Then we learn of Julian's experience of finding God in multiple ways:

—as above and beyond all that we know.

She explains this in a following chapter, where she says: Jesus Christ is both God and man. And as regards the Godhead, he is himself highest bliss, as it was in the beginning and shall be without end. And this endless bliss may never be increased or diminished in itself. . . .This was shown abundantly in every Showing and especially in the twelfth, where he says: "It is I who am the highest" (31).

—and within our hearts

—also as the one we worship: for example, in community prayer and shared sacraments

—as the one revealed in the reading of the Scriptures and the teachings based on them.

And, for her, as the one revealed in these showings.

Again, an unspeakable joy seals her certainty that it is God who speaks and is present to her.

And for us?

At times we may find God in the works of creation—from the simplicity of the flower and the leaf to the flickering of the distant star, knowing that God is the being of all.

More often, perhaps, we know that God is within our hearts, shaping our desires and our delight.

Or we know, simply by the bent of our intention, especially in silence, that God is.

At all times, even when prayer seems least satisfying, we know that it is God whom we serve in daily living and in prayers of the church.

God's grace is fitted to us like a garment. We understand that God is in all, and we love the God who is in all, according to our own gifts, and according to the help God offers us.

God asks no more.

A Deed Will Be Done

Our Lord God showed me that a deed will be done.
He himself will do it.
I shall do nothing [regarding this deed] but sin.

—but my sin will not hinder God's goodness from working. And I saw that the *beholding* of this is a lofty joy in awe-
filled souls

—who evermore, in accord with their nature, by grace desire God's will.
This is the meaning of the words: "This deed shall be done by
me."

—that is, *by the general man—by all that will be saved.*
And though this word should be taken to mean that the deed
will be done by the general man,

—it does not leave out the individual.
For what our good Lord will do by means of his poor creatures—it is now unknown to me.

Chapter 36

COMMENTARY

We are not directly invited by Julian to enter into this mysterious prayer which she describes. But if we are led by grace to
do so, she assures us of joy.

She *beholds* only that a deed will be done which will bring it
about that "all shall be well." We can know nothing of the nature of this deed or when it will be achieved.

Looking carefully at Julian's words, however, we discover
that it is Christ and the members to whom he is bonded who
will bring about this blessed transforming of our miserable
condition into joy.

The wonder of it all is especially that, though the corporate
body of Christ will bring about the deed, individuals may also
play a part.

What individuals and by what means Julian does not know.
She does not want us even to speculate about these matters.

Somehow—by the power of Christ and his members—unhindered by sin, the promise that "all shall be well" will be fulfilled.

We may ask to share in Julian's own "beholding" here and to stand in awe also of the way individuals may be called on to bring the great deed into being.

Prayer for Amending Our Lives

Our courteous Lord shows an all-embracing friendship by
keeping us so tenderly while we are in sin.
Furthermore, he touches us most secretly
and shows us our sin by the sweet light
   —of *mercy*
   —and of *grace.*
Then when we see ourselves so foul, we think that God is an-
gry with us for our sin.
And then we are moved by the Holy Ghost
   —to *prayers of contrition*
   —and to *the desire of amending our life,* with all our strength.
  . . .
Then our courteous Lord shows himself to the soul, merrily
and with good cheer, and with a friendly welcoming. . . .
   "My darling, I am glad you are come to me. In all your woe
I was always with you.
    "And now you see that I love you
    And that we are bonded in bliss."
Thus are sins forgiven
   —in *mercy*
   —and in *grace*
and our soul honorably received
   —in *joy*
As it shall be when we come to heaven.

Chapter 40

COMMENTARY
It is easy to think that in sin we take the first step and go to
God asking for forgiveness. But Julian reminds us that it is
God who makes us aware of our sin.
   At the same moment when we are made aware of our sin
   we are also made aware that mercy and grace are offered to
   us.
    In prayers of contrition we change, but God does not.

For Christ assures us that he was with us even when we were not with him.

Joy floods our soul when we promise to change our sinful ways.

God shows us a welcoming face. Prayers of contrition are answered by new assurances of our bonding with Christ in love.

Living in Prayer and Longing

Then I understood truly that all manner of thing is made
ready for us
   —by the great goodness of God
to the degree that whenever we are ourselves in *peace and love*
   —we are, in fact, saved.
But since we may not have this in fullness while we are here
It behooves us always to live
   —in sweet *prayer*
   —and in lovely *longing*, with our Lord Jesus.
For he longs to bring us to the fullness of joy. . . .
God is *love* and teaches us to do as he does.
He wants us to be like him
   —in wholeness of endless *love*
     —for ourselves
     —and for our even-Christians.
Just as God's *love* for us is never broken because of our sin,
   in the same way God wills that our *love*
     —for ourselves
     —and for our even-Christians
   should never be broken.
But he wants us
   —authentically to hate sin
   —and endlessly to love *ourselves* and *others* as he does.
This word that God said is an endless comfort: "I keep you securely."

Chapter 40

COMMENTARY

As she does so often Julian asks us to consider two things at
the same time, in order to have wholeness and balance.
   We are still on pilgrimage longing for heaven.
   At the same time, we are to have confidence that we are already saved.
   This cannot mean, of course, that we can presume on our

salvation and take careless liberties with the way we live.

Nor does Julian teach that in some intense moment of feeling we reach out and take Jesus for our Savior and that by an act on our part we are saved.

We are already saved to the degree that we are

—in *peace*

—and in *love*.

But given the complexity of life it is difficult to know our own state with regard to these dispositions.

Are we in true *peace* with others

—or merely dominating them?

—or tolerating them?

—or submitting to the domination of others for our own comfort?

—or quietly being co-opted into going along with what we should have the courage to challenge, even though the consequences would be unpleasant?

—or really keeping our hearts at peace because we make decisions in God's presence?

Harder yet to answer is the extent to which we really live in *love*. But we have some directives.

The pattern of our *love* is God.

This, of course, must have some limitations, as the creature cannot love as fully as the *God who is love*.

—We can, however, try *to love those whom God loves*.

—Here, in particular, we try to love *ourselves*.

What is it in ourselves we are to love? How is love for ourselves different from obnoxious self-centeredness and egotism? How can love for ourselves counter the self-loathing that may follow sin, or the guilt that may cling to the conscience even after conversion of life?

—And we try to love all our *even-Christians*.

How can this be when we do not always know who is in God's love and who is not? (Julian will deal with this at another time). How can we love those who seem to seek to destroy the tender shoots of goodness that we are fostering in our own lives? How can we truly love others without being an enabler who unwittingly sustains others in their self-destructive ways?

Such questions we should ask one another in prayer and study to determine, as best we can, what it is to love.

—Also we can try to love *endlessly* as God does, not allowing our love for ourselves or for others to falter or break off.
This is how God loves. Not even sin can break off this love. This is hard to believe, since it goes contrary to the way we incline to act.
In this loving which perseveres despite sin, offenses, and rebuffs, we have to meet the challenge not to condone and pamper weaknesses and irresolution in ourselves and others.
—Genuinely, authentically we are to detest sin.
—Endlessly we are to love those whom God loves.
To live this way we need prayer.
And we need to keep our sights and our hearts on what is to come.
With Julian we try to rest in God's comforting assurances without taking God's care for granted like an ungrateful friend.
We are bidden to keep our hearts on what is prepared for us—the great joy which is to come.
We do not separate longing and prayer.
They are a way of life for us.

We know the experience already of sharing with others the same desire for a good gift which we expect.
—Even the coming of springtime, for example.
—Or the arrival of a long-absent family member.
(How endless the interval between the first sighting of the airplane that brings that person and their safe approach to where we stand!)
—Or comfort for a people struck by natural disaster or im-

prisoned in poverty or war.

— How easy it is to join prayer and longing, in companionship with others, when we are of one mind as to what will bring happiness.

We stand in all of life sharing a great longing with Jesus— for the fullness of joy.

We don't even know what it is that awaits it. But we pray.

Part of our "sweet prayer" is to hear in our hearts God's words of comfort.

"I keep you most securely."

JULIAN: The Fourteenth Showing

Two Conditions for Prayer

After this our Lord showed me about prayer.

In this Showing [the 14th] I saw that there are two conditions our Lord intends for it.

—one is that we pray *aright*;

—the other is that we have unwavering *trust*.

But oftentimes we do not trust completely, for we are not sure that God hears us, as we think

—either because we are *unworthy*

—or because we *feel* absolutely nothing.

—for we are as sterile and dry oftentimes after our prayers as before.

And this, in our feeling and our folly, is the cause of our weakness.

At times I have felt this way myself.

Chapter 41

COMMENTARY

Julian first takes up the second condition for prayer: trust.

She understands, from her own experience, what undermines trust:

We tend to ask how God can listen to the prayer of someone like us

—unworthy, as a weak creature

—unworthy, as one who has sinned

—unworthy, as one who has taken God's gifts for granted before

—unworthy, as one who does not even know how to pray.

And we ask if God *does hear* our prayers. If God hears us,

—why do we not feel the warmth of another's presence, as we do when we open our hearts to one who understands our plea?

—why do we not have confidence that God's strength will be with us?

—why do we not feel as if God holds our hand, pouring comfort into our being?

—why do we seem to be saying words which we do not fully believe, asking for graces which we only half-heartedly want to be given us?

Julian has been through all this, she says.

We can think about her, at the window of her cell, listening to the stories of others who felt this way, too. We can tell her our story.

We need greatly to trust.

More About Trust

Our Lord brought all of this [about trust] suddenly to my mind, and said:

"I am the ground of your beseeching.

   —first, it is my will that you should have it;

     —and since I make you to want it

     —and you do ask for it,

how should it then be that you should not have what you ask?"

And thus, in the first statement, with the three formulations that follow, our good Lord showed a mighty comfort, which the words clearly convey.

And in the part where he says: "And you do ask for it," he shows a very great pleasure, and the endless reward he will give us for our petitioning.

And in the part where he says: "How should it then be that you should not have what you ask?" he is indicating that this is impossible.

For it is a most impossible thing that we should ask for

   —*mercy* and *grace*

and not have it.

For all these things that our good Lord makes us to ask for, God has already ordained to give to us from the beginning.

"I am the ground."

Chapter 41

COMMENTARY

Having exhorted us to trust, Julian now explains why we have *reason* to trust that what we ask for will be given.

She introduces a teaching which will keep recurring: that the ground—the foundation—of our prayer is Christ himself.

   —Our prayer arises from Christ with whom we are bonded. Our prayer is like the movement of the waves out of the sea, like the springing forth of new growth from the earth, like the new leaves on the vine. It is the

Christ-life in us which gives rise to the stirring that is prayer. By fostering this prayer and not smothering it out, we earn God's good pleasure and our own endless reward. These prayerful desires (which) Christ has planted in our hearts will come to fulfillment. How could it be otherwise?

But what are these desires? Do they really relate to our daily life and the needs we feel as suffering human beings?

In Julian's sense of "mercy and grace," yes.

For *mercy* means all of Christ's work in restoring humanity. Hence, we may ask for relief from all the effects of sin—from all that comes from our limitations and the limitations of others.

And *grace* means all the work of the Holy Ghost in bringing about the effects of the Incarnation in our lives. And so we may ask for a deeper sharing in the Christ life.

Mercy and *grace* are at work—not just in what we perceive as sacred and holy—but in all aspects of our lives.

We may rightly ask, then, for all that makes us more fully human and for all that is promised through the Spirit. God's goodness—not ours—assures that prayer will be answered.

"I Am the Ground"

Here we may see that our *beseeching* is not the cause of God's goodness.

He showed that in truth in those sweet words where he says:

"I am the *ground*."

Our good Lord wants this to be known by his lovers on earth.

The more that we understand this, the more shall we continue to *beseech*, if we take it *wisely*.

This is what our Lord intends.

Chapter 41

COMMENTARY

Julian continues to draw conclusions and solace from the key truth: "I am the ground." Christ is the rich earth, the substratum, the hidden stream that enables us to pray and assures that our prayers will bear fruit and not be sterile stocks drying in the wind. God's goodness—not ours—assures that prayer will be answered.

Julian is here also emphasizing what it means to take this teaching *wisely*. She is not discounting the teaching of the learned who are wise, for she herself draws on such sources. But she does not permit such limited wisdom to displace what flows from the source of wisdom, the Christ-Mother. In this she is solidly based on the Scriptures.

For example, the psalmist stands at ease before God, even in that widely-used, sorrowful prayer of repentance, the *Miserere*:

Still, you insist on sincerity of heart,
and in my inmost being teach me *wisdom* (Ps. 51:8).

Persistently Julian urges us to come face to face with God as Wisdom, as far as it is possible in this life. She begs us not to focus on her as a teacher either, but "wisely" continue to look to God (Chapter 8). She wants us to try to grasp something of what is meant by the fact that our bliss is endless, lasting forever. "Think also *wisely* of the greatness of this word 'ever,' for in that was shown a high understanding of love, with the manifold joys that follow from the passion of Christ . . . and that he made us to be his crown and endless bliss" (Chapter 23). She seems to try to dissuade us from *looking to God to give us* what we want in limited, specific ways rather than praying that in each case the kingdom of God will be realized: "If I should act *wisely* in accord with this teaching . . . I should not be disturbed over any manner of thing, for 'All shall be well'" (Chapter 35). The very disclosure of Christ in the Trinity is as "the *Wisdom* of the Father" (Chapter 51). But, when we, like the Adam of the parable of the lord and the servant, come to see our loving Lord clearly and learn to see our true self rightly, then we are in the way of wisdom: "When these two are *wisely* and truly seen, we shall have rest and peace here in part and the fullness of the bliss of heaven" (Chapter 51). The very image of God in ourselves focuses on wisdom:

> Before he ever made us, he loved us. And when we were made we loved him. And this is a love [by which we are]:
> —made of the *goodness* of the Holy Spirit.
> —empowered in our reason by the power of the Father;
> —and *wise* in our mind by the *wisdom* of the Son.
> And thus is the human soul made by God, and in the same moment, knit to God (Chapter 53).

Julian's profound words here may also be read in the light of a passage from St. Paul (1 Cor. 2:4–5):

> . . . my message and my proclamation were not with the persuasive [words of] *wisdom*, but with a demonstration of spirit and power, so that your faith might rest not on *human wisdom* but on the power of God.

The Prayer of Beseeching

Beseeching is a *new, gracious, lasting* will of the soul
   —united and fastened to our Lord's will
      —by the sweet, inner working of the Holy Ghost.

Chapter 41

COMMENTARY

The prayer of beseeching is that form of prayer which responds to the directive: "Pray always."

It is to live in the presence of God, with a will and desire shaped by what God has made us for. It is the direction our life takes. The beseeching prayer does not require constant awareness, only constant will.

   —This will and desire and direction is ever new:[3] that is, it is reborn and made real in every breath, in each successive heartbeat.

   —It is *gracious*: that is, it is the work of grace in us, the work of God dwelling within us.

   —It is *lasting*: that is, it links the moments of our life one to the other until our death. It is *lasting* in that this beseeching prayer will find its reward in the joy of heaven.

In other places Julian joins "new and lasting" to stress her vision of both time and eternity. She says in Chapter 14, concerning the bliss of heaven: ". . . it shall last forever, as new and delightful as when it was first received." Those who pray by directing consciousness to each breath, or each heartbeat, become aware of how our relationship to God is "ever new."

What Happens to Our Prayers?

Christ himself is the first one to receive our prayer, as I see it.
>—And he accepts it with much thanks and with great rejoicing.
>—He sends it up above and places it in safe-keeping where it shall never perish.

It remains there before God and before all the saints
>—continually being received
>— and always helping us in our needs.

And when we shall enter into our bliss
>—it will be given to us for an increase of our joy
>—and with the endless gratitude of God.

Chapter 41

COMMENTARY

How few things in this life last and bring us ongoing satisfaction!

But prayer is not among those things which pass away.

A parent will save over the years the child's first art work. A lover or a friend will save letters which speak of ongoing devotion. Collectively we save the writings, music, and art of gifted and creative persons.

Mother Christ, our friend Jesus, puts our prayers in the treasury where the saints see them and where we shall see them again, to our endless delight.

Christ assured Julian that he remembered the service of her youth—the living prayer of her life of love. He remembered the three prayers she had offered in less-enlightened days—before the Showings.

One of the joys of heaven will be to see in some way all the best intentions and the loveliest prayers that we and all who will be saved have entrusted to Jesus' hand.

>—All the prayers we have offered for our own needs.
>—The petitions we have made for others.
>—The thanks and the prayers of wonder which have

arisen in our hearts when we read the Scriptures or med-
itated on the beauty and the fruitfulness of nature.

—The prayers of trust and longing for the city of God.

In times of loss and dashed hopes we can cling to the
knowledge that the best part of our life lasts.

When it seems to us that we cannot pray, we have the
prayers of the past "always helping us in our needs."

We can make prayer even of the swift awareness that the
moment of Christ-like living will last. We can say to ourselves
when "the hurtling days" seem "to pass without a murmur or
a mark":

Make something of this moment!
Let it live through awareness
That its pulse will beat still
When the day itself is dead.[4]

Prayer Changes Us

Glad and merry is Christ over our prayer.
He awaits it, and he wants it.
For with his grace
   —he makes us like to himself
      —in our hearts
      —as we already are in our humanity.
This is his blessed will.

Chapter 41

COMMENTARY

Jesus shows us in himself what humanity is capable of becoming.

If he did not first take on our human nature, it would be hard for us to imagine what it means for that human nature to be transformed.

But now we know, in part.

In him there is no arrogance. There is no self-centered isolation that seeks one's well-being at the expense of others.

In him there is no piety which serves as a mask for inaction.

He is never silenced by fear of what he may have to suffer by disturbing an unjust order.

But Julian will experience in the sixteenth Showing in a more striking way what it means to be like to Jesus in heart as well as in humanity. Then the nature of that change will become more clear.

Christ became human that we might become Christ-like.

He is glad and merry when we pray, bravely, to have a heart like his.

Pray Earnestly!

Here is what Christ says:
"Pray earnestly
　—though you have no taste for it, as you think.
"For it does you good
　—though you do not feel that it does;
　—though you see nothing;
　—yes, even though you think you are powerless.
"For when you are dry and empty, sick and frail, then your
prayer is most pleasing to me
　—though there seems to you to be little pleasure in it.
"And thus all your living is prayer in my sight."

Chapter 41

COMMENTARY

How hard it is to come before God with no more feeling than
a stone.

It is then that God urges us to pray, to pray with earnest attention, and to believe in the worth of our prayer.

Harder yet it is to pray when pain, sorrow, sickness, or fa-
tigue weigh us down, and we turn to prayer for comfort.

And we find none. Words and action seem pointless and
routine. God does not seem to know who we are or that we
are here.

Someone other than ourself is looking at our prayer and
putting a value on it, an even greater value because it brings
no perceivable reward: "Your prayer is most pleasing to me."

No time is lost. Living like this is prayer, as God sees it.

He Whom We Seek

Because of the reward and unending gratitude that you have
in store for us,
   —You desire to have us pray always in your presence.
You accept the *good will* and the *hard labor* of your servants, no
matter how we feel.
   It pleases you therefore that we *work* reasonably and with
discretion, by your help and your grace
   —both in our prayers
   —and in our right living
directing our *desire* toward you until we have you whom we
   seek in the fullness of joy.
He whom we seek is Jesus.
He shows this in the fifteenth revelation, where he says:
   "You will have me for your *reward.*"

Chapter 41

COMMENTARY

How do we make all our living into a prayer?

This is what Julian explains here.

We know that we can be praying whether we are giving
ourselves directly to prayer, or giving ourselves to daily work.

The daily work must, first of all, be "right living": working
with integrity, with purpose, with moderation, without ex-
ploiting others. The core of that work must be the desire to
find God, knowing that only God can give us unlimited joy.

We are often very conscious of what others think of our
work. It is also important to be conscious of how God, who
sees the heart, looks on our work.

The practice of "right living" is just as demanding as the
practice of prayer.

We wish to be taught by those who pray well, and that is
good. We need also to learn the complex art of "right living"
so that we are praying always, as God bids us.

Give Thanks and Enjoy

Thanking also belongs to prayer.
Thanking is a new, inward, knowing
   —accompanied with great reverence and loving awe
   —inclining us to do, with our whole strength, what the
   good Lord draws us towards;
      —and *inwardly*
         —to give *thanks*
         —and to *enjoy*.

Chapter 41

COMMENTARY

In the prayer of thanking, too, Christ is the ground of our praying, just as in beseeching.

Beseeching, as we have seen, is a fixing of the *will* on God and *desiring* what we need.

Thanking is *knowing* inwardly: it is like hearing music, or fixing our senses on the rising sun, or coming suddenly upon the good will of another. It fills us with awe as we acknowledge the goodness that is made visible. We rejoice in what we know inwardly.

We may be moved to thank God by returning to the place where we have been granted a gift of Divine presence or generosity. Or we may stand in a place where we know others have prayed and been blessed by God. Or we may perceive the loving ways that friends and family members—or even complete strangers—assist one another, knowing that it is the Christ-life within them that gives rise to their ways of acting. Thanking is *knowing* this.

It is then that we *know* inwardly how good God is.

Apart from prayer we may think of thanking as enjoying a gift and telling someone we are pleased with what they gave us. Or we may think of the giver and be glad that such a person chose to do something for us.

But thanking in Julian's sense focuses on the goodness of

the giver, a goodness that pours out on others—not just on ourselves—like the rays of the sun. This is like thanking the earth for being fruitful. It is like thanking a bird for sharing its song.

The psalmist often offers thanks to God. For example (92:2–3):

It is good to give thanks . . .
to sing praise to your name, Most High,
To proclaim your love in the morning,
and your faithfulness in the night.

Breaking Out Into Words

Sometimes, in its abundance, thanking breaks out into words, and we say:
"Good Lord, grant us mercy.
"Blessed may you be!"

Chapter 41

COMMENTARY

Though thanking is an *inward knowing*, it can also give rise to prayerful words and to song.

Often teachers of prayer suggest that we begin with speaking our prayer and repeating familiar words. Then after much practice, silent prayer takes over as our way of addressing and listening to God.

There is much truth in such instruction, of course. But Julian presents a different experience here: the silent, inner knowing of God's goodness and God's gift of salvation cannot be contained. Words are needed again—often the same familiar words with which we began the practice of prayer. They come back spontaneously, without effort on our part.

We do not become more spiritual by ceasing to use words. Julian does not teach us to strive for a "spiritual life," apart from our body. Rather, she draws us to a total life lived in the Spirit. Hers is not "a spiritual life," if that implies a putting away of human ways of acting. She draws us to life— transformed indeed—but still life as we know it.

Words are never adequate, of course, for telling about God. But words, as well as silence, signify that we want God to read our hearts and to inscribe wisdom and knowledge therein. This is especially true of those outbursts of short, familiar phrases that we have already made our own.

When the Heart Is Dry

Sometimes when the heart is dry and feels nothing, or else the
enemy is tempting us,
   —then *reason* and *grace* drive us to cry aloud to the Lord
      —recollecting his blessed *passion* and his great *goodness.*
Soon the strength of our Lord's word enters into the soul
   —enlivens the heart,
   —moves it by grace to its true activity,
   —and makes it pray blissfully and truly find joy in the
   Lord.
In God's sight praying thus is a blessed giving of *thanks.*

Chapter 41

COMMENTARY

Jubilation is not the only occasion for putting our prayers into
words. It is good sense and high wisdom to cry out to God
when our heart has no taste or feeling for prayer, and when
we are besieged by the lure of the unholy.

We can turn to the prayers we have learned, or reflectively
read the prayers we use habitually. Or we can create the
prayers that suit the moment.

We know that when we are sad, thinking cheerful
thoughts, or looking at beautiful scenes or art can overflow
into our whole being. We become like these thoughts.

We know that in anxiety and trouble, peaceful music—for
example, that which suggests the soothing sounds of the sea,
or the melodies of birdsong—can bring us calm. We know
that deep breathing, or rhythmic walking, can shape our inward feelings and bring peace. In such ways outward be-
havior can create our inward dispositions.

Julian describes her way of using exterior actions to get
control of her inner life when her heart feels stale and storm-
tossed. She calls on her good sense, strengthened by grace, to
move from lethargy to delight. Her way is to go over the story
of the passion such as she would find it in Luke 22:1–46. She

may have used the prophetic picture of the sufferings of Christ in Isaiah 53:3–12. To recall God's goodness she may have made use of the prayer, called "The Magnificat," or "The Canticle of Mary," in Luke 1:46–55.

The word is a bearer of grace. Take, for example, the words in the epilogue of the book of Revelation (22:16): "I, Jesus, sent my angel to give you this testimony for the churches. I am . . . the bright morning star."

—Our heart finds new vigor from such words.

—Our whole being turns towards love, for which we were made.

—We pray joyfully, as the meaning of the words takes root in our will and even in our feelings.

This is true thanking.

Three Teachings About Prayer

Christ Jesus wants us to have a right understanding of three things that pertain to prayer:

—the *first* is "by whom" and "how" our prayer springs forth.

—He explains "by whom" when he says, "I am the ground" [of your beseeching]

—And he explains that "how" is by his goodness, when he says, "First, it is my will" [that you pray].

—the *second* concerns "in what manner and how" we should use our prayers.

—that is, that our will should be turned towards the will of God, *enjoying*

—which is what he means when he says: "I cause you to will it."

—the *third* is that we are "to know the *fruit and the purpose* of our prayer":

—which is that we be made one with, and like to, Christ in all things.

The whole of this lovely lesson is meant to teach us this, and this is its purpose.

And Christ Jesus will help us

And we will make our prayer just the way that he says.

Blessed may he be forever!

Chapter 42

previous

COMMENTARY

In the last chapter, Julian named praying aright and having unwavering trust as two conditions for prayer. She has already told us about trust.

Now she is ready to teach us what it means to pray aright. This can be achieved in part by having a "right understanding" of those things that pertain to prayer.

The whole revelation, which she calls a "lesson," is intended to teach us to pray. For the most part the lesson is like a series of reflections on what she sees and hears and what happens to her.

But at this point she offers a little outline of the lesson. She also shows in two examples how to recall the parts of this outline by relating each part to what Christ says.

The third part of Julian's instruction also needs some word which Christ speaks. We can find our own in the Scriptures.

One source is in Christ's instructions to the disciples at the Last Supper (Jn. 15:5):

I am the vine,
you are the branches.
Whoever remains in me and I in him
will bear much fruit. . . .

And further on, while praying to his Father for the disciples: "That they may be one, as we are one" (Jn. 17:22).

There are available in our time many new instructions on prayer—some useful, some tangential to the meaning of prayer. We can test these instructions by asking where and to what degree they add something to Julian's three-part overview:

1. Does the prayer embody the truth that Christ is its ground?
2. Does it turn our desires and intentions toward God?
3. Does it produce the fruit proper to prayer, making us one with, and more like to Christ?

These are crucial tests.

Obstacles to Trust

For this is our Lord's will: that our *trust* be as great as our prayers.

—for if we do not *trust* as much as we pray

—we do not fully honor our Lord in our prayer

—and also we delay, and distress ourselves.

And the reason for this is, I believe,

—that we do not truly realize that our Lord is the *ground* from which our prayers arise.

—and also that we do not realize that prayer is a *gift* to us from his love.

For if we really knew this, we would *trust* to receive

—as a *gift* from our Lord

all that we desire.

Chapter 42

COMMENTARY

Why do we not trust as we ought, but rather pray half-heartedly? Julian here links together some of what she has said about *trust* and about *praying aright.*

In *praying aright* we realize that Christ is the *ground* of our prayer. It then follows that prayer is a *gift* from the goodness of God.

With such belief we are able to *trust* that we will receive also the *gift* of all that we truly desire.

God Gives Before We Ask

No one of us ever asks, I am sure, with a right intention,
  —for *mercy and grace*
Unless *mercy and grace* are first given to us.

                                             Chapter 42

COMMENTARY

Mercy refers here to the work of Christ as mother:
  —He is our mother in taking our human nature on himself.
  —He is our mother in mercy in the ways in which he works within us.
    —In him we grow and develop, like the child in the womb.
    —He reforms and restores us, countering the evil which arises contrary to goodness.
    —By virtue of his passion, death, and resurrection, he unites our scattered, divided self to our most inward Self, where God dwells.
Grace designates the work of the Holy Spirit, working with mercy.
  —The Spirit *rewards* us, giving us recompense for what we suffer and for our labor.
  —And the Spirit also *freely bestows gifts* on us, beyond anything to which our labors could lay claim (Chapter 58).
Mercy and grace, then, refer to Christ and the Holy Spirit touching everything in us and in our lives: our eating and drinking, our sorrowing and hoping, our speaking and dealing with others.

We can therefore pray for anything that is good, anything that we need, because *mercy and grace* enable us to do so. Before we pray they are already with us.

A Temptation Against Trust

But sometimes it comes into our mind that we have prayed a
long time
And yet, it seems to us, we do not have what we prayed
for.
But at such times—I truly believe this—we should not be
discouraged. For it is certain that our Lord intends for us to
keep on waiting
—either for a better time
—or for more grace
—or for a better gift.

Chapter 42

COMMENTARY

Many of Julian's insights and experiences are for us a matter
of faith alone. But here, in this passage, we all find our experience—the experience of seeming to pray in vain.

We learn over time to tolerate patiently the lack of a visible
answer to beseechings that ask for gifts for ourselves—better
circumstances, better well-being, improved family relations.
About these we can learn to say that the time is not right, or
that a better gift may follow.

It is most difficult, however, to pray for what does not center on ourselves, or those near to us, and still see no sign of
change for the better.

We pray for peace in a violent world, and in the very midst
of peace, violence breaks out again—with death, destruction,
hatred, greed.

We pray for an easing of poverty, and nations take up war
against the poor, to aggrandize themselves.

We pray for fidelity and light among Christians, and many
more seem to fall away into lives apart from God.

We pray for unity among separated churches, and the lines
of separation seem to harden and ossify.

In the midst of such prayer, coming from like-minded peoples, our patience and our faith are sorely tried.

It is then we must wait for a better gift.

There are signs, in small ways:

—Those who labored prayerfully for the protection of the earth against carelessness felt the tragedy of oil spills. But then they saw young people on the oil-soaked shores washing birds, gently, lovingly.

Who would have expected a self-centered generation to do this?

Here is a story from *The Roll*, a publication devoted to people who share their experiences in prayer:

When he died, they thought that the cross was the end of him, that all their hopes had vanished with him in the tomb. . . .The next morning they awoke to the terrible realization that it was to be the first day of a lifetime without him. . . .

But even as they mourned him, something was in the process of happening that would change their world. . .

Despite all the odds against it, Easter was on the way.

Resurrection

Sorrow . . . has to be handled like one waiting for a resurrection. It cannot be rushed. We cannot plunge headlong into joy completely on our own initiative. Sorrow, even that which comes from ordinary days, must run its course.

What can we do? We can, if we so choose, abandon ourselves to the mysteries and confusions of life by allowing those very mysteries and confusions to empty us of our limited perceptions and fill our emptiness with the certitude that there is more to life than the "obvious," that life, the divine miracle of miracles, pulsates with answers to questions we have not even asked.

After a searing tragedy, our professor "assured us with great conviction": "God is able to create out of darkness and chaos, but not one of us can rush creation. All we can do is stand close by one another and wait for light to come."

Years later, after a "dry spell" in my life, I stood with a friend on a beach waiting for the sunrise. We . . . were tired of talking. Suddenly, the first rays of light appeared on the horizon, and we watched the edge of night become the edge of morning. In some unfathomable way my friend and I understood that it was part of us. That fleeting moment, long past, survives in us still.[5]

This Is a Better Gift

What God wants for us is the *knowledge* that God is *being*.
God wants our *understanding grounded* in this,
 —with all our powers
 —with all our concentration
 —and with our entire purpose.
And on this *ground* God wants us to stand firmly and thereon
to set up our dwelling place.
 Then by the gracious *light* which is truly God, God wants
us to have an *understanding* of the things that follow from this:
 —the *first* is our noble and excellent *making*
 —the *second*, the price and worth of our *restoring*
 —and *third*, concerning all things that are beneath us:
  —that God has made them to *serve* us
  —and that God *keeps* them by love.
God means all these things as if saying in these words:
 "See. I have done all this before you began to pray;
 "And now you *are*, and you are praying to me."

Chapter 42

COMMENTARY

"On this *ground* he wants us to stand firmly and to set up
thereon our *dwelling place*." Here we stand and stay.

 This is the better gift that God may hold in store for us
when he seems to us to delay in answering our petitions.

 This is how we are to pray, to escape from under the despondency of not seeing our prayers answered.

 We are not to take refuge in railing against God, nor
dwell on our unworthiness as if some one more holy
might win from God what we seem unable to obtain.

 We are to move ever more deeply into a knowledge of
who God is and who we are.

 We are to think about our creation, and the gifts of the

new creation, and the riches of creaturehood surrounding us, they too made by God and endlessly kept in his love.

—Did Julian, in her own bouts with despondency, listen to the bird song, revel in the rain drops dripping from the eaves, think about the sea over which gifts from other lands came to her?

She is back to the vision of the little thing like a hazelnut, which is really all things, made, sustained and loved by God. . . .

She is back to Mary, who saw herself so little in the light of the greatness of God.

She sees into the profound truth that God is, and is the being of all things.

We are to try to understand this all-encompassing truth . . . we are to concentrate on the being of a single creature, and we are to direct our purpose and intention toward this understanding.

She here leads us back to Moses coming ~~down~~ from the mountain, asking God's name: "I am the one who is."

The mystery of it is that this seems to be "a better gift" which follows on our disappointment or dejection at not receiving what we ask for, when we want it, and in the way we want it.

While waiting for God to do something else, we first rejoice in all that God is now doing, trying really to understand what it is that God does, how God is the ground and foundation of all that exists.

Like a child's breath that is the "ground" of the soap bubble, so, in a distant analogy, God's breath is the energy that keeps things in being. . . .

I have been here awhile, God says. I have been taking good care of my creation. I love this creation. Now you are here.

And you have something to ask me.

God is here like a parent who has been here before we were born, preparing a place for us, with good gifts, and happy hopes.

Who is the God to whom we pray? The one who is.

"Where were you when I founded Earth?
Tell me, if you have understanding" (Job 38:4).
"Have you ever in your lifetime commanded the morning and shown the dawn its place. . ." (Job 38:12).
"You know, because you were born before them,
and the number of your years is great!" (Job 38:21).
"I had heard of you by word of mouth,
but now my eye has seen you" (Job 42:5).

We are to seek God, knowing that the things of God are ours, too—to serve us . . . and to show forth God's active love.

Julian does not tell us to quit praying for what we have asked—for the health of a parent, or the freedom of a prisoner, or the end to a drought.

But she tells us to pray aright, seeking first to know our God and ourselves.

God Does All

Now what Christ means is that we ought to know that *the greatest deeds are already done.*
—as holy Church teaches.
And in the *beholding* of this
—with the giving of *thanks* we ought to pray for the *deed that is now being done,* namely: that he *rule over* us and *guide* us in this life for his own glory and *bring us to his bliss.*
And this is why God has done all.

Chapter 42

COMMENTARY
The deeds already done are those which Julian has just listed: God created us, restored us in Christ, and created all else besides, to serve us (Chapter 42).
She tells us again to gaze intently on these deeds, *giving thanks* for them.

But there is a great deed yet to be done. In part, it is known only to God: "This is the great deed ordained by our Lord God from without beginning
—treasured and hid in his blessed breast,
—only known to himself,
—and it is the deed by which *he shall make all things well*" (Chapter 32).

Hidden in this deed, not yet accomplished, is the secret of how all will be well, despite suffering and sin—in fact, these were somehow necessary and bring to humankind some benefits in the end. *Sin was behovable.*

And there is another deed, which is being done now, and it is this one Julian wants us to pray for, *beseeching*:

It is made known in the mystery of the gardener/servant, who tilled the soil to bring forth fruit for the great lord. This is the mystery of Christ, who is at work in this life drawing us into union with God.[6]

This is the deed we know as the death and the resurrection of Jesus, re-enacted repeatedly in our own lives
—reconciling us to God
—directing us in the details of our life
—leading us on our pilgrimage to bliss.
We give thanks to God who has done all.

Behold God's Deeds and Pray

And God means also that we both
  —see that God does [all]
  —and pray to him for it to be done.
Now one without the other is not enough.
  For if we *pray* and *do not see* that he does it,
    —we become despondent and doubting
      —which is not to God's glory;
  Or if we *see* what he is doing and *do not pray*
    —we fail in our duty. And let this not be. . . .
But if we see that God does all and pray for it too
  —this brings glory to God
  —and profit to us.

Chapter 42

COMMENTARY

Beholding or seeing that God does all requires that we *beseech* God to do in our lives the deeds that belong to divine goodness.

We fail in *trust* if we do not *see* that God is indeed doing what we ask for.

We fail in praying aright—in completeness—if we do not *beseech* God for the deeds that we know God has designed and is doing.

We may be attracted to thinking about the mysterious works of God while remaining unaware of our own needs. Or we may feel that we must rush into making petitions for our needs without calling to mind that God does all before we ask.

We are here instructed to make our prayer complete: *beholding* and *beseeching*.

The "deed that is now being done," as Julian has told us, is God at work in our lives drawing us into union with the Trinity. If we do not pray for this, it will not be done. The mystery of Christ's death and resurrection will not come to be in our lives. Though our prayer does not cause God to give us grace, our failure to pray may prevent those graces from being realized in our own lives.

God "sees" us in our despondency, which proceeds from blindness. But God does not "see" us when we merely know about divine mysteries and do not correspondingly pray. In such a case the divine gaze is not on us, as it were, and our empty "seeing" is sterile and bears no fruit. Such is the case of those who are superficially but not realistically *wise*.

Julian's wisdom is to bridge with prayer:

—what we grasp—intellectually or intuitively—of God's ways;

—what we know we should do by way of prayer so that God's ways will bear fruit in our lives; and so that our prayer will exist forever in the divine beholding.

In practice every true prayer of *beholding* involves an earnest act of *beseeching*, perhaps with some of the petitions of the Our Father, either in the form of words or of silent desire.

Beyond All Understanding

Everything that Christ has ordained to do, he wills that we
pray for it
    —either in *particular*
    —or in *general*.
The *joy and the bliss* that this is to him
and the *thanks and the honor* that this will be to us:
These surpass the understanding of all creatures, as I see it.

Chapter 42

COMMENTARY

We cannot grasp the mysteries of the universe, in its greatest
or smallest forms. Much less can we comprehend the consequences of prayer: the honor to God, the bliss accruing to
ourselves.

Sometimes it consoles us to lay before God a particular
need. But we are here assured that it is also profitable merely
to ask in general for all that God ordains to do in the members
of Christ's body, the church. "Christ, have mercy" suffices.

A Definition of Prayer

For prayer is a *right understanding* of the fullness of joy that is
to come
> —with intense *longing*
> —and unwavering *trust*.

Falling short of the *joy* that we are by *nature* ordained to,
makes us to *long*;
True *understanding* and *love*, with a sweet *remembrance* of
our Savior, by *grace*, makes us to *trust*.

Chapter 42

COMMENTARY

Here is the core of Julian's teaching on prayer: a definition,
which sums up what she has been explaining to us about the
conditions of prayer and its components.

"Right understanding" springs from our reason and from
our faith.

> —True understanding, Julian tells us in Chapter 6, leads
> us to pray to the goodness of God and not to use
> "means" apart from that goodness. It is to know that
> Christ is the ground of our prayer and wills that we
> pray, and to know that God is the being and goodness of
> all things, as she often reminds us.

"The fullness of joy" that awaits us is Jesus, our heaven.
The bliss that we are made for is also a share in the very rejoicing of Christ himself: humanity brought into glory
through the Son and a sign of his victory.

It is in our very nature to desire our own perfect joy—not
just as an abstract object of intellect and will, but as the fulfillment of our embodied selves. Such perfect joy requires also
that others, too, find what they long for.

> —Because we lack such joy, we go on desiring it.

By the gift of grace—by the Holy Spirit—we have confidence that prayer will be answered.

Grace is like bodily healing, which is beyond our power,

and yet is not accomplished except by our working in conformity with nature. Grace works with us, not without us.

—Our part is to keep our thinking straight; our longing in
conformity to the ground of our being, Christ; and our faith
rectified, by turning our reflections on Jesus, who rec-
onciles us with God.

Christ Can Ask No Less

Christ *beholds* us continually in these two workings [of long-ing and trust]
>—for this is our duty;
>—and in his *goodness* he can ask no less of us.

It is proper to us to work diligently in this way? And when we have done all that is asked, then we shall still think that it is nothing
>—and in truth it is nothing.

Chapter 42

COMMENTARY

This little passage calls to mind the Gospel parable of the use-less servant, who only does his duty, and is promised no spe-cial praise for it.

It also recalls what was said above about the sin of not praying: God beholds us in our prayer—but our failure to pray is not a deed which comes into his presence. . . .

We are here partners in God's deed. God enables us to do what we do. Hence we deserve no special praise. Nonetheless, we receive God's thanks.

No doubt we have often asked: *Why should I pray?* Is not prayer only a form of useless magic which fails in its effects? I pray for health, and I am still ill. We pray together for good weather, and our land is still devastated. Why, then, should we pray?

We pray, for one thing, because God tells us to. Prayer is a duty, a duty laid upon us by God's goodness. Why, then, should we fail to pray?

"We Shall Find All in God"

When we do all that we can,
and truly ask for *mercy* and *grace*
   All that we now lack, we shall find in God.
This is what God means with the words:
"I am the *ground* of your beseeching."

Chapter 42

COMMENTARY

We do what we can: These words give us peace, when we feel how weak our own efforts are.

What we can do is to ask in the right way for mercy and *grace.*

   —We reflected (in Chapter 42 above) on what *mercy* and *grace* mean in Julian;

      —*Mercy* is the work of Christ as mother.

      —*Grace* is the activity of the Holy Spirit, working with *Mercy.*

The *ground* of our beseeching is the meeting place of the divine at the center of our souls—the energy from which the Christ-life grows.

Summing Up

"I am the *ground* of your beseeching."
And thus in this blissful saying, along with the showing,
I saw that all our *weakness* and all our *doubt-filled fears* will
be fully *overcome*.

Chapter 42

COMMENTARY

Here we reflect, not only on the fact that Christ is the *ground of
our beseeching*, but also on the consequences of that fact.

—This is the basis of our *trust*, that what we ask will come
to be. It is our own weakness that threatens to overcome us,
but we have the power in Christ to deal with our weakness.
The Epistle to the Colossians (1:9–12) offers a similar assurance, when we pray for others:

[We] do not cease praying for you and asking that you
may be filled with the knowledge of his will through all
spiritual *wisdom* and understanding to live in a manner
worthy of the Lord, so as to be fully pleasing, in every
good work bearing fruit and growing in the knowledge
of God, strengthened with every power, in accord with
his glorious might, for all endurance and patience, with
joy giving thanks to the Father, who has made you fit to
share in the inheritance of the holy ones in light.

Christ
the Foundation
of Prayer

What Prayer Does

Prayer makes the soul one with God.
For though the soul is ever like to God
  —in *nature and substance,* restored by grace,
it is often unlike God
    —in its *condition*
      —because of sin on humanity's part.

Chapter 43

COMMENTARY

We might look at two rose bushes of the same species, but one is drought-ridden and diseased, while the other is fresh and healthy. It is not their species that makes them unlike, but their condition. This condition of unlikeness can be changed by the gardener, who can place them in good soil and expose them to water and light.

In ways that are mostly hidden from us, we are like God— in our nature and in our very being.

God's workings—of truth, wisdom, and love—are one with the perfect divine being.

Our workings fall short in truth, wisdom, and love—the condition of sin. Our substance (our centeredness in God) is out of touch with our changeable being.

The effect of prayer is to bring these workings—of truth, wisdom, and love—into such harmony with our whole being that we grow in likeness to God.

Prayer helps us to avoid sin and overcome its ravages. Sin is not in our nature, but in the present condition of that nature. That is why we are at the same time like to and unlike God.

Further Effects of Prayer

Prayer, then, bears witness
  —that the soul wills as God wills;
Prayer comforts the conscience
And enables us to receive grace.

Chapter 43

COMMENTARY

We pray not only to receive what we ask for, but to present ourselves to God saying, in effect: "Thy will be done."

Our conscience needs comforting at times when we are torn between two ways of acting, both of which seem equally desirable, or even at times, each mixed with evil. Julian needed such comfort when she felt she should desire an end to her life in order to be with God, but yet a continuation of her life in order to give honor to God, and especially to offer help to others.

As we continue to pray we become more receptive to grace and thereby find a peaceful way of coping with life's frequent dilemmas.

"Partners" in God's Good Deed

Thus, God teaches us to pray
And greatly to *trust* that we shall have what we ask.
For God beholds us in *love*
And wants to make us *partners* in [Wisdom's] good deed.

Chapter 43

COMMENTARY
The good deed here refers to that deed explained in Chapter 42: It is to be brought about by God ruling and guiding us in this life so as to bring us to bliss.

We become *partners* with God
—when we work and pray in consonance with the divine will,
   —the will which desires compassion, creative use of energies, and care for one another;[1]
—and also when we do the *works of God*
   —named for us, for example, in the beatitudes (Blessed are they who hunger and thirst for justice . . . who feed the hungry . . . instruct the ignorant . . .)
—and do all our *works in God*
   —shaping our ordinary life with integrity, joy, interchange with others.

All by God's Gift

God moves us to pray so that what is pleasing to God will be
done.
And for these prayers and the good will that we have
    —by God's own *gift*,
we will be *rewarded* and given endless *recompense*.
And this was shown where God said: "And it is you who
pray for it."

Chapter 43

COMMENTARY

"And it is you who pray for it" was said more fully in Chapter
42: "See, I have done all this before you began to pray; and
now you are, and you are praying to me." All was done before we were made, yet our prayer is somehow part of what is
done.

"All this" refers to the making, restoring, and keeping of
humanity, and the making and keeping of all things else, for
our delight and service.

Here, as so often in Julian, we are given the double perspective of time and eternity, interwoven.

    —It is not that time is unimportant in the light of eter-
    nity.

    —Rather, time is important because of eternity.

Julian repeats, in brief, ideas now familiar to her listeners:
It is in the very texture of daily life that we pray for what God
is doing and wants to do. Our daily living is part of our
prayer, which has its just reward; and our prayer and living
also receive a recompense beyond that just reward.

"What Could Please Me More?"

"And it is you who pray for it."

In this word God showed much pleasure and great delight:

> — as if greatly beholden to us for every good *deed that we do* (and yet it is God who does it);

And *because we pray to God* to do all the things [Wisdom] desires,

It is as if God said: "What could please me more than for you to pray to me fervently, *wisely*, and intently, to do the thing that I shall do?"

And in this way the soul by prayer is brought into accord with God.

Chapter 43

COMMENTARY

Here is God's supreme courtesy: that we are invited to become part of the good that is done.

On our part, what a simple prayer: to ask God for all the good that lies hidden in the divine plan—in the potential of each person, and in the potential of peoples, working in groups.

> —the *good* God wishes to do in our lives and in the lives of others—in those who sorrow, in those in prison, in those who prosper, in those in positions of power.
> —the *good* God desires to do in the times in which we live.

> This could be a time when liberty spreads among many peoples on Earth, when many are drawn to interior prayer, when compassion for the hungry and the homeless takes deeper root. Let us pray that these things be done.

This Is an Exalted Prayer

But when, by his grace, our courteous Lord shows himself to our soul,
> —we have what we desire.

Then, for a time, we do not care about praying for anything.

For all our powers of concentration are fixed wholly on *beholding* him.

And this is an exalted prayer, beyond our conceiving, in my view:

For the *purpose* which leads us to pray is now all fused into *seeing and beholding* him to whom we pray
> —marvelling and enjoying,
> —with reverent awe,
> —and with such great sweetness and delight in him
> —that we cannot *pray* at all, except as he moves us to do

during that time.

Chapter 43

COMMENTARY

What more is there to desire, if one beholds God, even within the limits to which we are subject in this life? What more is there to pray for?

We are still to pray for the fullness of the company of heaven, for heaven's plenitude.

This is what Christ longs for. Julian speaks of it as the "spiritual thirst," continuing the physical thirst on the cross:

The thirst of God is to have all humanity within himself; by this thirst he has drawn to himself the holy ones who are now in bliss; and as he gets these living members by his thirst, he is still drawing and drinking, and he still thirsts and longs (Chapter 75).

The bliss of heaven is not just our bliss, but the ending of the pain and sorrow of others. Hence, though we may want to take our rest in the felt presence of God, Christ leads us again to pray—to beseech that others, too, may come to bliss, and that we may come to bliss more fully.

When We Do Not See God . . .

I know well that the more a soul sees of God the more it desires to see, by God's grace.

And when we do not see God, then we feel a need and a reason to pray

    —because of what we now lack

    —and to prepare ourselves for Jesus.

Chapter 43

COMMENTARY

Here Julian recalls to us a theme from her general definition of prayer (Chapter 42), where it is said: "Falling short of the joy that we are by nature ordained to makes us to long."

    —If God seems present to us, we long to see what is still withheld.

    —If we are in darkness, we long for what we lack.

But again, seeking is as good as beholding, as Julian has already taught us. And, in truth, we are always seeking.

A Time to Pray

When the soul is *tempest-tossed, troubled,* and left to itself in *unrest*

then is the time to pray, and to make oneself *pliable* and submissive to God.

For there is no prayer whatsoever that makes God *pliable* to us

—for God's love is always the same.

Chapter 43

COMMENTARY

How succinct Julian is here. We ask the wrong question if we lament, "Why does God not hear me?"

We pray, rather, that we may hear God.

When we are troubled, empty, torn by the storms of life, then especially we should pray:

—not only to become more patient

—but also to love in a more dynamic way.

"Seeing No Other Needs . . ."

Thus I saw that:

> —whenever *we see needs* for which we should pray,
>> —God is there *following us*
>> —and *helping our desire;*

> —and when, *seeing no other needs,* we of his special grace plainly behold him,
>> —then *we follow God*
>> —and God *draws us into the Divine Self* by love.

For I saw and I felt that God's marvellous and overflowing *goodness* fulfills us in all our powers.

Chapter 43

COMMENTARY

In this passage Julian confirms her teaching on two modes of prayer:

> —*beseeching,* assisted by an active desire on our part;
> —and *beholding,* marked by spontaneous understanding.

God leads us sometimes into *beseeching,* sometimes into *beholding,*

> —and the prayer of *beholding* enables us more and more to love.

God at Work in All Things

I saw next that God's continuous working in all manner of *things* is done
  —so *goodly*
  —so *wisely*
  —and so *powerfully*
that it surpasses all that we can imagine, or know, or think.
  And then we can do no more than *behold him*
    —with a high, mighty *desire* to be completely made *one* with him
      —*centered* in his dwelling place
      —*finding joy* in his loving
      —and *delighting* in his goodness.

Chapter 43

COMMENTARY
Here is how a friend of Julian's sums up what she says here:

Thus prayer is a participation by the human will in God's will to manifest Himself in redeemed humanity. And it is increasingly a direct grasp by the centre of the soul of that Centre where all lines of our partial desires and petitions converge: the Centre of the world process which is Its revelation.[2]

Even in This Life

Then we shall, *with his sweet grace,* in our own meek,
unceasing prayers,
—come into him *now in this life*
—by many secret touchings of sweet spiritual insights
and feeling, measured out to us to the degree that we
can bear it in our simplicity.
And this is accomplished, and shall be, by the grace of the
Holy Ghost
—*until we shall die* in longing for love.

Chapter 43

COMMENTARY

And above all these ghostly sights is the direct but un-
intelligible touch of God. For God is the end and perfection of
prayer. Prayer, in its highest form the prayer of experienced
union, is thus a veiled foretaste of the perfect and unveiled
possession of God in heaven.[3]

Julian implies this connection between the experience of
coming to God now in this life and the possession of God in
heaven. A poet of our time captures this linkage:

Walk till you hear
light told in music that was never heard,
and softness spoken that was not a word.

The soul grows clear
when senses fuse: sight, touch and sound are one
with savor and scent, and all to splendor run.

The smothered roar
of the eternities; their vast unrest
and infinite peace are deep in your own breast.[4]

Not in This Life

No one can see God in this mortal life and live.

But when God, *with a special grace,* wills to be revealed
Then God strengthens the creature above the self, and measures out the showing according to the divine will as it is profitable at that time.

Chapter 43

COMMENTARY

Julian joins many other teachers about prayer who say that God is never fully revealed in this life: such a light would snuff out mortal life.

But she gives witness to special graces by which the creature is gifted with some passing experience of God.

She does not try to describe or explain this experience, only
    —that God makes it possible for her to do something she could not ordinarily do;
    —that the experience is what helps her at the time.

By the Spirit's Gracious Leading

God judges us on our natural *substance*, which is always kept one in him, whole and safe forever.

—and this judgment is *fully right*.

The human creature judges on our changeable *sensuality*, which seems now one thing, now another, depending on which part is drawn on, and on what shows outwardly.

—and this judgment is *mixed*.

The first judgment, which is of God's righteousness . . . is that fair, sweet judgment that was shown in all the fair *revelation* in which I saw him assign to us no manner of blame. . . .

But I could not be at ease in the beholding of this alone, because of *the judgment of holy Church* which I had understood before and which was continually before me.

And by this judgment I understood that I ought to see myself as a sinner, and by the same judgment I understood that sinners sometimes deserve blame and wrath. . . .

Then this was my desire:

that I might see in God how the judgment of holy Church in its teaching on this point is true in God's sight,

and how it is fitting for me to understand it, in such a way that both the revelation and the teaching of the Church are preserved, so that it is to God's honor and also the right way for me.

And I had no other answer but the wonderful example of a lord and a servant, as I shall relate hereafter.

But yet I stand in desire, and shall until the end

—that I might by grace know these two judgments as they pertain to me. . .

The more *understanding* that we have of these two judgments

—by the *gracious leading* of the Holy Ghost

The more we shall see and know our failings.

And the more that we see these failings, the more *by nature and grace* we shall long to be fulfilled with endless joy and bliss.

Chapter 45

COMMENTARY

Sometime back (Chapter 41), Julian explained that prayer has two conditions: we are to pray *aright*; and to have complete *trust*.

She is now ready to teach us more about what she means when she says that we are to pray *aright*.

Praying aright, she shows, is in part a matter of the understanding.

—We must *understand rightly* how God beholds us.

—We must behold ourselves and others with rectitude.

This involves some difficult points:

—God sees us in our substance, that is, in our very sharing in the divine life, as God wants us to be and as we shall be in heaven.

— We see in ourselves and in others only our sensuality, which means in the Showings all that we directly experience as our ordinary self, in body, memory, feeling, action, and thought.

Marvelously, this *sensuality* which Christ took as his own is the city of God. It is that part of Christ which suffered for the salvation of humanity.

By mercy and grace we gradually grow into seeing ourselves from God's viewpoint. But meantime our failings loom large.

Julian knows how heavy-hearted we are in the face of these failings—ours and those of others.

She takes this into consideration in her definition of prayer, which we can review here: "the right understanding of the joy that is to come" with intense longing and complete trust. This longing becomes more intense because "we fail of the bliss we are ordained to."

We know well enough how the sight of sins and failings can deter us from prayer, filling us with fear and discouragement.

But, rightly used, this awareness of our failings should increase our longing for happiness and hence help our prayer. This can happen, though, only if we *rightly understand* how God looks on us in our sin.

So the other condition for prayer—to pray aright—concerns Julian here.

This part of *right understanding* was very difficult for Julian—and perhaps more so for us. How can we assent to the lesson of the Showings—that God never looks on us with wrath or blame—and also adhere to the church's teaching that as sinners we deserve blame and wrath?

In some way both of these judgments are true. The parable of the lord and the servant (Chapters 51-54) helped Julian to reconcile these seeming opposites. It will help us, too. But, even thus enlightened, Julian continued to desire to know more about this mystery, these judgments so hard to reconcile.

So far as prayer is concerned, this is what Julian perceives:

—With the help of the Holy Spirit we grow in understanding of how both these truths apply to us.

—This grace deepens our awareness of our sins and failures.

—But instead of inspiring fear and despair, this deeper understanding heightens our longing for the bliss without end.

Thus we are brought back to the definition of prayer: a right understanding of that joy which is to come, with *intense longing* and unfailing trust. And failing of the bliss that we are ordained to, by nature makes us *to long*.

The sight of our sins is a most painful falling short of that bliss.

"But, Lord, to whom shall we go?"

So we turn again to prayer.

Knowing Our True Self

In our passing life which we have here in our sensuality, *our true self* is not revealed to us. . . .

We can have some knowing of our *self* in this life . . . but we can never fully know ourselves until the final moment, when this passing life with its pain and woe shall have an end.

And therefore it is appropriate for us
  —both by nature and by grace
to *long and desire* with all our strength
to *know our self* in the fullness of unending joy.

Chapter 46

COMMENTARY

Our *sensuality*—that part of us which can suffer—lets us see and experience our individual, sinful self; and this is salutary. Being aware of our sinful, weak self helps us to fear God, to be in awe of God, as we should be.

Similarly important is the effort to know our true self: the true self is known to us in this life by faith. Our individual self is transformed and transcended but never lost or absorbed:

But how. . . is this self transcended? First, the individual self is transcended when it recognizes its oneness—without loss of individuality—with the collective self that is the body of Christ. Secondly, not the reality of the self, but the relationship sustained by the self, is transcended. Only the "I" in which the sparkle of divinity is enmeshed resounds: Christ lives in the self, the self lives in God. In no way is this a loss, but only a fulfilling.[5]

This is part of the bliss we are to long for, which is at the heart of Julian's definition of prayer. We desire to know our self, wherein Christ truly makes his dwelling.

Peace from the Indwelling God

I felt within myself five kinds of workings, which are these: *enjoying, mourning, desire, dread,* and *confident hope.*

enjoying, for God gave me *understanding and knowing* that indeed it was himself that I saw.

mourning—and that was for my weakness.

desire—and that was that I might see more and more of him, all the while *understanding and knowing* that we shall never have full rest until we see him truly and clearly in heaven.

dread—for it seemed to me in all that time that the sight would go away and I would be left to myself.

confident hope, and this was for the unending love, in which I saw I should be *kept in his mercy* and *brought to his bliss.*

And the *enjoying* of this sight with the *confident hope* in his merciful keeping gave me such feeling and comfort that the *mourning* and *dread* were not greatly painful.

Yet in all this I beheld in this showing from God that the sight of him cannot be continuous in this life. This is both for God's honor and for an increase of our endless joy.

And thus we often fail to have sight of him and at once we fall back on ourselves.

And then we have no feeling of being right, nothing but the perversity that is in ourself,

—both that which comes to us from the *old root* of the first sin

—and that which comes from *our own devising.*

And in this we are travailed and tempested with the feeling of our sins and with pains of many sorts, in our spirit and in our senses, as we all experience in this life.

But our good Lord, the Holy Spirit
    —who is *endless life, dwelling in our soul*
    keeps us most securely,
    creates peace within us,
    brings comfort to us by grace,
    brings us into harmony with God,
    and makes us compliant to him.

And this is *mercy,* and this is the *way* on which our Lord
continually leads us as long as we are in this life
    —which is always *in flux.*

Chapters 46 and 47

COMMENTARY

While Julian is aware of the presence of God, she is filled with
joy, desire, and hope—feelings strong enough to soften her
sense of her own weakness and her fear that her sight of God
would fail.

Then she describes vividly what happens when she falls
back upon her self. At those times she has "no feeling of being
right"; she suffers in mind and body, as we all do, she adds.

In an act of *faith* she recalls that the Holy Spirit dwells in
her soul, helping her prayer.

Turning again to her *reason,* she reminds herself that life is
always in flux. It is in this very real world of confusion and
change that Christ is our *way.*

An Inward Cry for Help

I cried inwardly with all my might, seeking help in God,
meaning this:
    O Lord Jesus, king of bliss
    How shall I be set at rest?
    Who shall teach me and tell me what I need to know
    if I cannot at this time see it in you?

Chapter 50

COMMENTARY

This troubled prayer is Julian's cry to God for help in her dilemma over reconciling God's goodness and the blame the
sinner incurs. We may share in her dilemma. Or her struggle
may remind us of what we experience when new perspectives
from religious truth come to us—whether from theology, the
claims of the mystics, or through changes in science and culture. These new perspectives may seem to challenge the way
we have always construed our faith, or the way it is formulat-
ed by religious authority.

For our guidance, Julian was not concerned about a theory
or an abstract point of theology. She wanted to know how to
live—how to discern good from evil. As a help she turns both
to reason and faith. We can learn from her to have faith in
whatever is true, leaving it to God to show us, if need be, how
seeming opposites fit together.

To understand this matter helps her *to pray aright.*

It does not appear that she really puts this anguished cry
into words. But afterwards she could tell us in words what
her interior cry meant.

She shows us here how to pray from the heart, and with
the heart, when we are greatly troubled.

This is the point in the Showings where she reports on the
parable of the lord and the servant and her long reflection on
its significance. That parable puts her heart somewhat at rest,
and is in part the answer to her prayer.

Knowing Our Own Soul

If we are to come to know our own soul
   —communing with it
   —and conversing with it
We must seek for it within our lord God
   —in whom it is enclosed.
And I saw truly that it is necessary for us to be
   —in longing
   —and in penance
until such time as we are led so deeply into God that we really
and truly know our own soul.

Chapter 56

COMMENTARY

This passage draws on what Julian has already taught us: that God is the ground of our being and of our prayer.

God is in our soul and our soul is in God. The true self is this soul, at its point of union with God. We do not really know ourselves except by knowing God.

This perspective on life was discovered in our own times by the mystic Etty Hillesum, who learned to overcome despair and hate in the midst of mass murder under the Nazis. She indeed communed and conversed with her own soul:

> The significant struggle for peace and justice is the wrestling with oneself: to reach out for the divine powers hidden at the depth, resist the destructive impulses in one's own life, and help other people, as friend and counselor, to discover the source of new life in the *ground of their own existence.*[6]

Our continuous prayer of longing for God will bring us to know this true self, which shares in the compassion of the divine. Perhaps this knowledge for us will be only at death. Sometimes we are moved to say, when people die, "Now they know the great mystery." We seem to be standing outside, waiting at the door of the dark unknown.

Here a poet-mystic imagines herself standing at that door:

> . . . when fact arrests me at that solemn door,
> I reach and find the keyhole still too high,
> though now I can surmise that it will be
> light (and not darkness) that will meet the eye.[7]

Some Great Gifts of Prayer

In our spiritual birth [Christ] acts more tenderly in keeping us, without any comparison, inasmuch as our soul is of the greater worth in his sight.

    —He kindles our understanding

    —He directs our ways

    —He puts our conscience at ease

    —He comforts our soul

    —He lifts up our heart

    —He gives us, in part,

        knowing and *loving* of his blessed Godhead.

        With gracious *awareness* of his sweet manhood and his blessed passion.

        With courteous *marveling* on his high, transcending goodness.

Making us to love all that he loves, for his love, and to be pleased with him and all his works.

And when we fall, he quickly raises us up, by calling to us with love and by touching us with grace. . . .

For he—and he alone—is all power, all *wisdom*, and all love.

May he be blessed!

Chapter 61

COMMENTARY

This passage gives us a rare insight into Julian's most profound experience of prayer: knowing and loving the blessed Godhead, here in part, as it will be in fullness in heaven.

As the *ground* of our prayer the Christ-Mother works in all the ways listed here, in ways that encompass the whole of our praying and living.

We are to be aware of the Christ-Mother, both in the flesh and in the Trinity, never forgetting the passion, always being conscious of the divine goodness. In this light our will and desire continue the prayer of *beseeching*, and the understanding, the prayer of *thanking*.

The image of Christ as mother helps us to *trust*.

If we have a short prayer like Julian's, natural to us as breath, it will rise from our hearts and into words here.

Some pilgrims, journeying by bus on the hairpin curves of a road in the Swiss Alps and coming again and again upon new scenes of breathtaking beauty, found themselves saying in chorus: "Oh!" Julian's "May he be blessed!" is like that. Each fresh revelation of God's goodness stirs her to pray spontaneously, more absorbed in what she sees than in the words she uses.

Have Mercy on Me!

Oftentimes when we fall and our wretchedness is shown to us, we are so much afraid and so greatly ashamed of ourselves, that we scarcely know which way to turn.

In such times our courteous Mother [Christ] does not want us to run away: he would loathe nothing more than that.

Rather, he wants us to act like a child: for when it is distraught or frightened, it runs hastily to its mother for help with all its strength.

So Christ wants us to do, acting like a meek child and saying thus:

"My mother, by nature

"My mother, by grace

"My ever-loving mother

   "Have mercy on me.

"I have made myself filthy and unlike to you.

"And I may not, nor cannot, make amends except with your secret help and grace."

Then if we do not feel ourselves at ease forthwith, we can be sure that he is acting like a *wise mother*. For if he sees that it is more to our profit to mourn and to weep, he permits this, with sorrow and pity, until the time is right,

   —*out of love.*

He wants us then to conduct ourselves like a child, continuing naturally to trust in the *love of the mother* in weal or woe.

Chapter 61

COMMENTARY

Though Julian encourages us to pray to Mary as a revelation of the supreme work of creation (after the humanity of her Son), she instructs us here to pray to Christ himself as mother.

We are to keep in mind that in Christ as mother is the motherhood of the Trinity in all its properties:

   —Christ in the creating Trinity is mother by *nature*, mother of our "kind."

—Christ in his flesh-taking is our mother by grace, one with us in our humanity, and restoring us from the effects of sin.

—Christ in sending us the Holy Spirit to guide us in love is our mother in all that we do.

It is without fear or distrust, then, that we pray to this Christ-mother in words that ask for mercy.

We come with an *understanding* and *will* ever growing in *wisdom*; but with a *trust* as simple as that of a child.

Mother Church Is Christ Jesus

[Mother Christ] wants us to take ourselves mightily to the *faith of holy Church* and find there our *ever-loving mother*
— in the comfort of true understanding in communion with all the blessed ones.

> For *one person* may sometimes be broken, as it seems to that individual
>
> But the *entire body* of holy Church was never broken, nor ever shall be.

Therefore, it is a safe thing, and a good and a gracious, to choose, willingly and firmly, to be sustained by, and united with, our mother, holy Church
— that is, Christ Jesus.
For the food of mercy that is his cherished blood and precious water is plentiful
— to make us fair and clean ...
It is his office to save us ...
He wants us to love him, sweetly,
and *trust in him* meekly and firmly.
This is what he showed in those grace-filled words:
"You are ever secure in my keeping."

Chapter 61

COMMENTARY
Mother-Christ is also revealed here as Mother-Church, to whom we cry out for mercy and comfort.

In *communion* with one another, we are to find security.
— First, because the church visibly performs those functions which Julian listed (Chapter 61) as coming from Mother-Christ. The male Christ is mother: both men and women are to carry out these maternal tasks for one another in a maternal spirit.

—Second, because the church as the body of Christ is strong and secure, whatever be the weakness of individuals within it, and our own frailty.

We can get a sense of this communal strength by observing certain individuals who may be praying here and there before or after a liturgical service. We become aware of the vibrant faith of the broken-hearted, the bereaved, or the thankful as they commune with God. We share in that strength. Here is Mother Church.

The Eucharist, which is the food of mercy, is the way by which the Christ-Mother nourishes us and knits us into one body.

In this prayer we listen: Christ assures us that he whom we do not see is known to us in the church. Here we are completely safe, in Christ's hands.

Prayer for Healing

As truly as sin is unclean,
it is likewise unnatural.

And thus sin is a horrible thing for the beloved soul to see,
when it wants to be all fair and shining in the sight of God
    —as both *nature* and *grace* teach.

But let us not fear—except insofar as fear may profit us.
Rather, let us make humble complaints to our beloved Mother
[Christ].

And he will sprinkle us all over with his precious blood
and make our soul pliable and mild and *heal* us beautifully in
the course of time.

Chapter 63

COMMENTARY

In the church the Christ-Mother also does away with the sin
we deplore when we pray to be free of its effects.

    —Sin is contrary to our nature, depriving it of its whole-
    ness and beauty.

    —Humbly we pray to Mother-Christ for healing, especially
    with regard to the blindness that leads to sin, and with re-
    gard to the paralysis and immature willfulness that are im-
    ages of sin.

Julian also signifies sin under the image of poor, worn,
soiled, or ragged clothing:

    —Christ hid his divinity under the poor cloak of our im-
    poverished humanity.

    —The Christ-Adam (Christ united to our humanity)
    wore a tunic of shreds and tatters, made of a scanty
    piece of poor cloth, short like a worker's garment,
    stained by sweat.

    —On the cross the robe of his humanity—his flesh—was
    bloody and torn and sagging under the soil and on-
    slaught of sin.

We pray, with *trust*, to Mother-Christ to clothe us anew, in bright clean garments, lovely enough for the company of Christ and his holy ones.

Christ in his return to the Father wears a glorious robe, ample and colorful and full of beauty. Thus the robe of his humanity shares in his glory. *— began p.62*

This is the end of the long fourteenth Showing, which began with teachings about prayer. Here we pray *aright*, when we pray for healing and for a new beginning in grace. We pray with *trust* when we appeal to Mother-Christ like a child—with the *trust* of a child.

A Blessed Contemplation

It is a sovereign comfort and a *blessed beholding* in a loving
soul,
    —that we shall be taken from pain.

[handwritten margin note: Ah; i like my drawing of being uprooted from ange soi !]

    For in this *promise* I saw the marvelous *compassion* that our
Lord has for us in our sorrow, and a *courteous pledge* of complete deliverance.
    For it is God's will that we be *comforted* in superabundance,
as is shown in these words:
    "You will come up above,
    "And you will have me for your reward,
    "And you will be fulfilled with joy and bliss."
    It is God's will that we concentrate on this *blissful beholding*
as often as we can;
    And, with the help of grace, keep ourselves therein as long
a time as we can.
    For this is a *blissful contemplation* for the soul that is led by
God, and greatly to God's honor for the time that it lasts.

                             Chapter 64

COMMENTARY

In our sorrow and our pain it is not easy to think of God, for
we are greatly absorbed—by the very nature of our suffering—in ourselves. Julian does not here ask us to rejoice in
our pain but to look forward to the day when it will be no
more.

Julian understands well the self-absorption that threatens
us in our pain:

> Though we are [sometimes] in such intense pain, sor-
> row, and distress that it seems we can think of absolute-
> ly nothing else but the condition we are in, or what we
> are feeling, as soon as we can, we are to pass over this
> lightly and count it as nothing (Chapter 65).

In our time, more than in Julian's, we have better ways of

controlling or defeating pain, and more psychological ways to cope with suffering. But even now we experience pain, loss, fear, and other forms of distress which are beyond our control. Julian does not ask us to "forget" our pain, knowing that to do so is next to impossible.

She offers us, instead, a simple way of *beholding*: we are to concentrate on knowing that we will be delivered from pain and find our reward in Christ. Our poor bodies and spirits, so constricted here, will be fulfilled in joy.

Pain and suffering sometimes seem like a punishment, and therefore just to be endured. But in her distress Julian saw the face of God filled with "marvellous compassion," not vengeance or reprisal.

We have, no doubt, seen people, even without the guidance of faith, use pain as a challenge. They discover a new kind of joy. Without denying the suffering, they rise above it, and find new potential in their inner life. One of many examples of this was a gifted man who from the age of fourteen needed to use a wheelchair because of muscular dystrophy. He spent much of his pain-wracked life fighting courageously and creatively for the rights of the handicapped. Now deceased, he has left the imprint of his life on legislation, in city ordinances, and in the ramps that now give the handicapped access to churches, schools, and public buildings.

Julian offers here a way of making prayer out of pain, by remembering that in the end:

"We shall be taken from pain."

Nor is this a low form of prayer: it is a *contemplation* to which we are moved by grace. We are counseled to use it often and for as long as we can, making it, if possible, a longing for the joy that is to come.

Julian assisted herself in this contemplation by the words to Christ: "You are my heaven." She also heard the promise: "I am your reward, exceeding great."

Desiring the Presence of God

When I speak of reverence, I mean a holy, courteous awe of
our Lord, to which humility is knit.

—This means that the creature sees the Lord as wondrously great

—and the self as wondrously little.

And these virtues are endlessly possessed by the beloved
of God.

This awe [that I speak of] can now be seen and felt to some
degree by the gracious presence of God, when it is experienced.

—[Feeling] this presence in all things is something most to
be desired

—for it brings about a marvellous confidence

—in true *faith*

—and unwavering *hope*

—and the greatness of *charity*

—with an *awe* that is sweet and delectable.

Chapter 65

COMMENTARY

Feeling at times the presence of God is an integral part of
growing in the Christ-life. We need to desire that experience
and to draw fruit from it when it is granted to us.

To this end we may recall Mary, the mother of God, at the
annunciation (Lk. 1:26–38). The awesome presence of God
filled her with faith, hope, and with that charity that made her
the mother of all the faithful:

O God,
you fulfill our desire
beyond what we can bear;
as Mary gave her appalled assent
to your intimate promise,
so may we open ourselves also
to contain your life within us,
through Jesus Christ. Amen.[8]

Etty Hillesum records her experience of the presence of God, shaped with the feeling that God is mother:

I had the feeling that I was resting against the naked breast of life; one could feel her gentle and regular heartbeat: I felt safe and protected.[9]

God's presence comes in endless variety.

Prayer in Time of Trouble

For God wants us to know:
> "If you *know* and *love* and reverently *fear* me,
>> —you shall have peace
>> —and be greatly at rest
>> —and whatever I do will give you much pleasure."

This is what our Lord showed in these words:
> "Why should it grieve you to suffer awhile,
> since it is my will and to my glory?"

Chapter 65

COMMENTARY

In time of trouble Julian does not have recourse to theory about the will of God and the purposes of God.

Rather, she hears the words of God directed to her while she is in a state of grief.

The words bring peace, though the grief remains.

The Height
and Depth
of Julian's Prayer

Prayer in Temptation

A little smoke came in through the door, with a great heat and a foul smell. I said:

—"O bless the Lord! Everything is on fire in here!"

I thought it was a real fire that was going to burn us all to death.

So I asked those who were with me if they smelled anything foul. They said no, they smelled nothing.

Then I said:

"Blessed be God!" For I knew then that it was the fiend that had come to tempt me.

And I turned at once

—to what our Lord *had shown me* that day,

—with all *the faith of holy Church,*

for I beheld that they were *both the same* [the Showings and the teachings of the faith].

And I fled thereto in search of comfort.

At once all faded away

And I was brought to great *peace and comfort*

—without any sickness of body

—or uneasiness of conscience.

Chapter 66

COMMENTARY

The parable of the lord and the servant showed Julian—though still mistily—how the teaching of the church and her own Showings—were both the same. In part, that resolved her difficulty over learning "that there is no wrath in God" and "God does not blame us in our sin," when the theological language of her time seemed to hold the opposite.

But it is one thing to solve a dilemma intellectually and it is quite another to silence the turmoil deep in our unconscious.

Julian experienced this ongoing turmoil in the form of a demonic temptation. More than once she was tempted to disregard the Showings and return to an earlier pattern of life. It came to her mind that just to concentrate on keeping out of sin was enough. But this would be to deny the Showings and their insights.

She describes what she did: she set her mind and thoughts again on what Christ had shown her, and she did so with an acceptance of faith. Throughout, she addresses herself to God with trust.

—She still relies on the test of experience—the appearance of fire—and at the same time she checks out the experience of others. She learns by this that the "reality" of the fire is not physical.

—She does not cast aside, out of fear, the religious experience that has brought her such comfort in revealing to her—and for the sake of others—truths about the goodness of God.

—Lastly, she looks again at that experience in the light of the faith that the community of believers accepts.

These steps put down the demonic temptation.

From then on she was at peace. Her conscience was set at rest.

However, she still did not fully understand. That is why she continued to contemplate the Showings, especially the great parable, for some twenty years.

There is nothing magical about Julian's recourse to prayer. It is intertwined with the weakness and limitations of the human condition.

A dilemma like Julian's occurs when we feel torn between a maturing commitment of faith and the patterns of faith from childhood; or between the call to a new commitment which seems to conflict with accepted patterns of action; or between taking an unpopular stand that may be judged as disloyal to friends, family, or institutions.

In prayer we can find the strength to decide such conflicts in peace.

Again, turning to Etty Hillesum we find a wisdom like Julian's in resolving conflict:

. . . she fully realized that religious experiences and religious language had to be examined critically as to their political and psychological impact. She realized that the search for God could be an escape from the uncertainties of a troubled world; it could be a subtle gesture of self-centeredness; it could be a spiritual alibi for not being in solidarity with those who suffer . . . an attempt to make concentration on God the wall keeping away the cries of the oppressed. . . . On the contrary, she found that the encounter with God opened her eyes to oppression and injustice in the world.[1]

Similarly, Julian went beyond a passive, simple-minded acceptance of the formulas of faith to brave encounter with the Lord of faith. Though, because she was a woman, her right to teach was in question, she passed on what she learned and experienced in writing and in counsel, to her even-Christians.

God in the City of the Soul

Then our Lord opened my spiritual eye and showed me my soul in the center of my heart.

I saw the soul as extensive as if it were an *endless world* and a *blessed kingdom.*

And from the kind of place it was, I understood that it is a *glorious city.*

In the midst of that city sits our Lord Jesus, God and man . . . . And I saw him clothed solemnly and gloriously.

He takes his place in the soul, in peace and in rest.

And the Godhead

—sovereign *power*

—sovereign *wisdom*

—and sovereign *goodness*

rules and guides heaven and earth and all that is. . . .

When the soul comes above all creatures into the self, it cannot stay there, beholding that self. Rather, all of its beholding is directed blissfully to God

—that God who is the maker, dwelling therein.

for in the soul of humanity is God's true dwelling place.

And the supreme light and the brightest shining of that city is the glorious love of the Lord, as I see it.

What could make us more fully have joy in God than to see what deep joy he has in his own works? . . . It is his will that our hearts be raised powerfully above the depths of this earth and above all vain sorrows and that we have *joy* in him.

Chapter 67

COMMENTARY

In this blessed showing Julian sees within herself the glorified Christ in union with the Godhead.

The members of the church form, with Christ, a glorious city. Here on Earth, as well as in heaven, Christ is "at home"—like a mother—in the soul of humanity.

That greater self—the individual in union with the members of the church—is a most desirable sight.

But the light of that city is the love of Christ.

—As the *source of light* Christ is regal.

—As the *presence of light,* penetrating everywhere, Christ is close to us.

Our prayer is *joy,* sharing in the joy that Christ himself takes in the transforming accomplished in heaven and now in progress on Earth.

The Fruits of This Prayer of Beholding

This was a delightful sight, and a restful Showing, as it will be without end.

Beholding this while we are here is most pleasing to God and benefits us.

—It makes the soul that beholds it to become *like to that One* whom it beholds.

—and through grace it *unites* the soul to God in rest and peace.

Chapter 68

COMMENTARY

"For in the soul of humanity is God's true dwelling place."

This is the sight which Julian bids us to contemplate. We can do so, of course, only with God's gift.

The experience always reveals God as mystery. Yet at the same time God's gift comes to us at a specific time and place and is connected with a specific event. According to Carl Jung, the unconscious is the medium from which such a religious experience seems to flow.

Many have thought that in the euphoria of a grand, collective event—perhaps in the appearance of a popular religious figure animating a crowd—they have encountered the divine mystery. But later it becomes clear that such an experience is ephemeral. A feeling of oneness with a mass of people is temporary and superficial. It lulls the consciousness rather than awakening it. A true encounter with the divine begins with the intensely personal. In turn, the deeply personal opens out to the whole of humanity, to a sense of bonding and connectedness. And because the encounter came forth in a context of a time, place, and particular event, the fruits of that encounter can touch our lives forever.

A certain woman, incarcerated for felony, planned to make this painful experience a continual memory in her life so that she would never repeat her mistake. She took with her, upon release, a small piece of the orange cloth in which the felons were clothed as her "image" of prison. So those who behold God dwelling in the soul of humanity, may treasure an evocative image or small token as a reminder of when and where this mystery unfolded at its fullest for them. As the square of orange cloth reawakened pain in the former felon, so such a token can reawaken the fruits of encounter with God. It may be that a hazelnut, or an intricate piece of lacework, served thus for Julian, keeping her in touch with feelings of awe, pain, joy, or emptiness.

It is a mystery, of course, as to how our religious experience is rooted in our impoverished or divided inner selves. Yet many have had experiences which strengthen the belief that God dwells in the depth of the spirit and that in that dwelling all are knit one to the other. These experiences are often interpreted within the framework of the individual's belief—or unbelief.

Those who share Julian's perspective will find much to reflect on. She sees Christ indwelling the human soul, in its oneness with others, and leading humanity on the way of love.

"Listen Attentively to These Words"

The Lord did not say:

"You shall not be tempest-tossed, you shall not be weary, you shall not be distressed."

But rather:

"You shall not be overcome."

God wants us to listen attentively to these words, and to be ever strong in firm *trust*

—in weal and woe.

For God loves us and takes delight in us, [saying]: "I want you to love me, to delight in me, and fully to *trust* me." *And all shall be well.*

Chapter 68

COMMENTARY

We can picture Julian giving this counsel again and again to persons who came to the window of her cell, with stories of trouble and doubt. We can entrust her with our own stories.

Always trust, she says.

"You shall not be overcome."

Trust with joy.

"And all shall be well."

Julian's prayer here is like that of some verses in Psalm 129 (1–2), speaking for the people of God:

"Much have they oppressed me from my youth,
    now let Israel say.
Much have they oppressed me from my youth,
    yet they have not prevailed."

Praying with Eyes, Words, and Heart

I heard tongues chattering, sounding like two people who were jabbering at one time—as if they were in a debate over some serious affair. It was all a low muttering, and I understood nothing of what they were saying.

All this was to drive me to despair, I thought, for it seemed to me as if they were mimicking the praying of beads, when they are recited loudly, lacking any devotional intention and the proper care which we owe to God when we pray.

And the lord God gave me grace greatly to trust in him, and to comfort my soul with speaking out loud, as I should have done to another person who was under duress. . . .

> I fixed my bodily *eye* on that same cross which had given me comfort earlier.
>
> I used my *tongue* to speak of Christ's passion and to repeat the creed of Christ's holy Church.
>
> I fastened my *heart* on God with all my trust and all my strength. . . .

Thus was I delivered . . . by the power of Christ's passion.

Chapter 69

COMMENTARY

This is Julian's account of being distressed.

She tells us how she *worked* at comforting herself:

—finding an object on which to fix her attention;
—repeating prayerful words which were familiar to her;
—fixing her heart trustingly on the God who had spoken to her so often.

In this way she is not overcome, and peace returns.

The aim of the demonic temptation was to force Julian to forego belief in her Showings and in her resolve to share them with others. Instead, the temptation strengthened her faith in the fifth Showing, in particular. In that experience she understood that all the fiend's power is restrained in God's hand, and she felt a strong desire that all her even-Christians see, with her, how evil will be turned into good.

Also With Contemplation

I understand that God's face has three expressions:

—In the time of our pain and our woe, he looks on us with the face which shows the passion and the cross, helping us by his blessed virtue to bear our suffering.

—In the time when we are in sin, his face shows sorrow and pity, keeping us safe and defending us against our enemies.

—These two are the common expressions which he shows to us in this life.

—With these two is mingled the third, and that is his face

—like, *in part*, as it shall be in heaven

—and that is a gracious *touch* and *sweet glimpse* of the spiritual life by which we are kept secure

—in *faith, hope, and charity;*

—and with *contrition* and *devotion:*

—and also with *contemplation*, and all manner of true consolation and sweet comfort.

The *blissful face* of our lord God brings about all this in us by *grace*.

Chapter 71

COMMENTARY

Whatever our condition we are all called to "see" God, even on Earth.

If we *pray rightly*, we see God's two ordinary expressions, present to us even in our sorrow and in our sin.

Sometimes there are glimpses of God's face of *joy*.

This third expression was granted to Julian in the first Showing, where she says: "Suddenly the Trinity fulfilled the heart most of joy. And so I understood it shall be in heaven without end to all who come there" (Chapter 4).

Distinguishing True from False Fear

All fears, other than reverent fear, that are set before us—
though they come to us under the mask of holiness—are not
as true.

And this is how we can tell them apart:

The fear that makes us flee in haste from all that is not
good,

and to fall onto our Lord's breast, like a child into the arms
of its mother, with a determined will and with our whole
mind:

—*knowing* our weakness and our great need;
—*knowing* his everlasting goodness and his blessed love;
—*seeking* him as our only salvation;
—*holding fast* to him with confident trust.

The fear that leads us to us act like this is *natural, gracious,
good, and true.*

Chapter 74

COMMENTARY

How we turn to God, how we pray, is offered here as a test of
false from true holiness.

Reverent dread makes us turn to God as mother.

We are praying *aright* if we know our need, if we pray to
God's goodness, and if we know God as the source of our
healing. We find such *right* knowledge by betaking ourselves
to the God who gives us birth and helps us to grow in *wisdom.*

We *trust* to have what we ask in prayer, because God is our
wise and loving mother.

Praying for Trust

Let us desire [these gifts]:

    —to *fear God reverently*

    —to *love God meekly*

    —and to *trust God greatly.*

For when we *fear God reverently,* and *love God meekly* our *trust* is never in vain.

The more our *trust,* and the stronger it is, the more we please and give honor to the God we *trust* in.

And if we fail in this *reverent fear* and *meek love* (which God forbid), our *trust* will be misdirected for awhile. Therefore we are in much need of *praying for trust* to our lord of grace

    —that we may have this *reverent fear*

    —and this *meek love*

      by his gift in heart and action.

For without this no one can please God.

                              Chapter 74

COMMENTARY

Returning to the theme of *trust,* Julian bids us pray for it, along with *reverent dread* and *meek love.*

The lack of *reverent dread* and *meek love* could undermine our *trust.* These are not merely dispositions of the heart but energies which shape our actions and our relations with our even-Christians. We do not trust, as if we were about to win at a game of chance, but we trust as part of our total relationship to God and others.

Reverent dread, meek love, and *trust:* these three are closely intertwined.

Praying to Keep from Sin

The soul that *beholds* the kindness of the lord Jesus beholds no hell but sin, as I see it.

And therefore it is God's will that we recognize sin; and God wills:

—that we *pray* earnestly

—that we *strive* deliberately

—that we *seek* for teaching meekly

so as not to fall blindly into sin.

And if we fall, it is God's will that we rise quickly, for the greatest pain that a soul can have, is to turn anytime from God by sin.

Chapter 76

COMMENTARY

Julian's view of hell develops with the progress of the Showings.

At first she thought of it as the dwelling place of the fiends. Then she considered it as intense pain, asking if the pain of Christ's passion was not like hell. No, her reason assured her, for there is despair in hell, and that is greater than all other pains (Chapter 17).

Later, she wished for a vision of hell, in order that she might be motivated to live a better life (Chapter 33). No such vision was given to her, but her reason was led to a deeper understanding. Sin, rather than hell, came into the center of her inquiring. Sin so destroys the confidence of sinners that they think themselves worthy only of the punishment of hell (Chapter 39). Sin is more vile and more painful than hell (Chapter 63), and by nature and grace we hate sin. If all the pains of hell were laid out before us, we should rather choose all that pain than sin (Chapter 40).

Her manner of praying has changed: from considering the pain of hell in order to avoid sin, by *beholding* the kindness of God she has come to such hatred of sin that even hell's pains would be preferable (Chapter 40). In fact, there is no harder hell than sin (Chapters 40 and 76).

So by *beholding* the goodness of God, we pray, work, and seek instruction so as not to fall into sin. If in our blindness we do sin—as we will—we return to God easily.

We are not counseled to keep the thought of hell before us, but rather to be more intent on recognizing sin.

Seeking Remedy in God

Anyone who wants to be at peace, when brought face-to-face with another person's sin
  —should *take flight* from it as if from the pain of hell;
    —seeking remedy in God for help against it.
  For looking on another person's sin creates, as it were, a thick mist before the spiritual eye;
    —and we cannot, for the time, see the fair beauty of God,
      —unless we look on these sins
        — with *contrition*, along with the sinner;
        —with *compassion*, for the sinner;
        —and with a *holy desire* to God, on behalf of the sinner.
  Unless we act in this way, the sins of others disturb, wrack, and hinder the soul that looks on them.
  I learned all this in the Showing about compassion.

Chapter 76

COMMENTARY

Midway in Julian's reflections she returns to the three petitions which had begun her journey of prayer. She now sees these as gifts which she will be called upon to exercise in relation to sinners. First she learned this about compassion:

> Thus I saw how Christ has compassion upon us because of sin. And just as before in the passion of Christ, I was filled to overflowing with his pain and compassion, similarly in this Showing [the thirteenth] I was filled in part with compassion for all my even-Christians, for that dear, dear people of God that will be saved (Chapter 28).

In the same Showing she learned that whatever kind compassion we have on our fellow-Christians, that is Christ in us. Looking harshly at the sinner is perilous. Instead of wishing to punish sinners, we are to look on them with *contrition*, for in some ways we are in complicity with the sins of others. (Our appetite for consuming what is satisfying spurs on the greed of the oppressor who, in turn, may deprive the worker of a living wage.)

Instead of harshly judging sinners, and shunning them, we are to let Christ's own compassion come to life in us.

Instead of considering ourselves better than other sinners, we lift them up to God in prayer. Our *desire* is a share in Christ's spiritual thirst, that all may come to him. To do otherwise is to barter away our peace.

Wisdom in the Creature

Wisdom in the creature is to act in accord with the will and counsel of our highest, sovereign friend.

—This blessed friend is Jesus.

—It is his will and his counsel that we stay near him and present ourselves to him, familiarly, always, no matter what state we may be in.

—For whether we are filthy or clean, we are all one in his love.

—He does not want us, either for weal or for woe, to take flight away from him.

Chapter 76

COMMENTARY

Those who are "not wise" in the lore of the learned have here a way to act with wisdom: to take counsel with the divine friend, Jesus, and act accordingly.

Julian urges us to present ourselves to him in prayer at any time, with no fear of being rebuffed.

A Temptation Against the Prayer of Beholding

Because, in ourselves, we are so changeable, we often fall into sin. Then, too, there are hindrances
—from the inciting of the enemy
—and from our own folly and blindness.
For this is what they say:

You know very well that you are a wretch, a sinner, and a deceiver. You do not do what you have been commanded. You keep on promising our Lord that you will do better, and then right away you fall again into the same sins, namely, into sloth and wasting time.

For that is the way sin begins, as I see it, for those creatures who have given themselves to serve our Lord by the *inward beholding of his blessed goodness.*
    This makes us afraid to appear before our courteous lord.
    It is then that our enemy will set us back with this false fear of our own wretchedness, and with the pain that he threatens us with.
    For it is his purpose to make us so despondent and so weary in this that we should put out of our mind *the fair blissful beholding of our everlasting friend.*

Chapter 76

COMMENTARY
In referring to hell Julian showed us how she moved from fear of pain and despair to *beholding* God's goodness as the way to avoid sin. Sin is the real hell, she tells us.
    Here she unmasks the false counselor who, enemy that he is, tries to discourage us with the sight of our sin. Such counsel is in reality the beginning of sin, eating away at the will to continue *beholding* God's goodness and *beseeching* the gifts of mercy and grace.
    Julian does not think of the beginning of sin, for the one

who seeks God, as pride and self-sufficiency. Rather, such a one is more commonly hindered by fear, low spirits, and concern over weakness and failure.

Why keep trying, the false counselor asks. You aren't getting anywhere with these prayers to God's goodness. How can you trust when you are so untrustworthy yourself? Are you not destined for the pain of hell?

This is the time to hasten to Jesus, the friend who teaches true *wisdom*. It is time again to *behold the goodness* of our everlasting friend.

Remain in This Beholding

Here, then, is the remedy [against the fiend and his company]: to be aware of our own weakness and to flee to our Lord.

—And the more prompt we are in this, the more we profit by drawing near to him.

And this is the sense of what we should say:

"I know very well that I have a malignant pain:

—but being *almighty* the Lord can punish me

—and being all *wisdom*, the Lord may punish me *wisely*;

—and being all *goodness*, the Lord loves me most tenderly."

And in this *beholding* it is necessary for us to remain.

For it is a lovely meekness in a sinful soul, brought about by *mercy* and by the *grace* of the Holy Ghost, when we willingly and gladly accept the punishment and the discipline that our Lord himself will give us.

Chapter 77

COMMENTARY

When Julian earlier described the prayer of *beholding*, it was a matter of joy and delight: God's continuous working in all manner of things—by power, wisdom, and goodness—inspired in her a great desire to be one with God (Chapter 43). Now in a new form of the prayer of *beholding* we are instructed to accept with patience the penance that is inseparable from our daily lives.

This advice puts a new face on contemplation. It is one thing to *behold* God's working when we see the beauty and rightness of God's active presence. It is quite another thing to find peace in God's working when we confront anguish, guilt, sorrow, confusion, and the cruel pains which burden us. And what if these pains are inflicted by the ill-will and malice of another? Can we realistically recommend this path of prayer to those who are abused by society and trampled down by the self-righteous and the greedy?

At such times we try to remember that the Christ-Mother to whom we betake ourselves transforms evil into good. And we rehearse the roles of *mercy* and *grace* centering on the passion.

Though what happens to us in life may seem like a punishment inflicted by God in anger, we are called to believe that God works only through love.

This, too, is the prayer of *beholding*.

Keeping in Mind His Passion

It was shown, in particular and in depth, and with a loving countenance, that we shall meekly and patiently bear and suffer the penance that God himself gives us:

—*Having in mind* his blessed passion.

For when we *keep in mind* this blessed passion, with pity and love,

—then we suffer with him, as his friends did who saw him. 〈? Didn't they flee or deny ?〉

This was shown in the thirteenth revelation . . . where he says:

Do not accuse yourself overmuch, protesting that tribulation and your sorrow are all your fault. For I do not want you to be imprudently despondent nor sorrowful. For I tell you, no matter what you do, you will have sorrow. Therefore, I want you to recognize your penance *wisely*, and then you will truly see that all of life is a profitable penance.

Chapter 77

COMMENTARY

This is how Julian's youthful prayer was answered, her petition to be present at the crucifixion with Mary and Christ's other lovers who were there. She was gently taught that in order to suffer with Christ, it was not required that she be transported in a vision to the historical scene of the crucifixion. It is not a matter of "looking on." Rather, life itself is Christ suffering in us.

To make this practical, it may help to find some episode or pain in the passion that is like our present pain—physical pain, mental anguish, apparent failure, betrayal by friends, separation in death, disbelief of our well-meant words, and, in general, a kind of loss-of-control over our movements and our lives.

Then we can suffer with Christ. These sufferings are a very real way of sharing in the experiences of the dying Christ.

Appended to this basic lesson, there is added a concrete way of comforting ourselves. When things go wrong in life, we wonder if we brought the pain on ourselves, whether by sin or folly. Someone may say to us: "Well, your motives may have been all right. But if you had only done things this way."

Clearly we are never completely free of some responsibility for what goes wrong, yet Christ says:

> For I tell you, no matter what you do,
> you will have sorrow.

He Will Teach Us How to Ask

Let us flee to our Lord, and we shall be comforted.

Let us touch him, and we shall be healed.

Let us hold fast to him, and we shall be secure and safe from all peril.

For our courteous Lord wants us to be as much at home with him as our heart can imagine or our soul desire. But take care that we are not so familiar with him as to forget courtesy. For our Lord himself, while being completely at home with us, is also fully courteous. He is courtesy itself. . . .

To become like our Lord: this is our very salvation and our complete bliss.

If we do not know how to do this, we should desire it of our Lord, and he will teach us.

—For it is what he wants, and it is to his honor.

"Blessed may he be!"

Chapter 77

COMMENTARY

Here is another occasion for the prayer of *beseeching:* to desire to become more like to Jesus

—and to be comforted, and healed, and safe from all peril.

We are at home and at ease with our courteous Lord, who is our intimate friend. But Julian warns us, in effect, that this familiarity does not imply that Christ is our chum or our buddy. It is not a relationship to be trivialized, nor despoiled of mystery.

The prayer of *beseeching* includes desiring to be taught how to pray for this need: to become more like to Christ.

—This means to think as Christ does, and to will as Christ does.

—But part of the mystery of the Incarnation is that Christ took not only our common humanity but an individual humanity in time and place and in particular circumstances.

—Only by prayer and study and mutual help can we begin to know what it means for our individual humanity—born in a different time and place and in other circumstances—to become like to Christ's. In this dimension, too, we have need of comfort, healing, and security from peril.

This is part of what our Lord may teach us in our *beseeching*. To show us how to balance familiarity and courtesy Julian repeats here her habitual prayer: "Blessed may he be!"

An Obstacle to Beholding God

How steadfastly God waits for us and never changes expression. . . .The person who is highest and nearest to God may see himself sinful, and in need, along with me. And I who am the least and lowest of those who shall be saved can be comforted along with the one who is the highest. Thus Christ united us all in charity, when I was shown that I should sin.

And for the joy that I had in the *beholding* of God, I did not give attention readily to that Showing.

Then Christ stopped at that point and would not teach me any further until he gave me grace and will to pay attention.

And by this I was taught, that though we are lifted up high into *contemplation* by our Lord's special gift,

—yet we need at the same time to understand and look on our sin and our weakness;

—for without this knowledge we cannot have true meekness;

—and without this meekness we cannot be saved.

And also I saw that we cannot gain this knowledge by ourselves, nor from any of our spiritual enemies, for they do not want for us so much good.

—If it were left to them, we should not have this knowledge until the end of our lives.

Thus we are much indebted to God who will, for love, show us our sin *in this time of mercy and grace.*

Chapter 77

COMMENTARY

So great is Julian's joy in her prayer of *beholding*, that she is loath to be aware of her sinful self.

Our charity for one another is based in part on knowing that we are all in need of comfort because of our sin.

Only in prayer do we gain knowledge of the sinful self, as well as of the deep self that is the core of our being. Here it is the sinful self that is unveiled—to our dismay.

But we need not be dismayed, even though we are discomfited. (For) *mercy* and *grace* still fill and direct our lives.

Praying *aright* involves paying attention to what we are really like, when God—perhaps even in the midst of our prayer of beholding—gives us light and will to do so.

Waiting to Receive Us

When we have fallen by frailty and blindness, then our courteous Lord touches us, moves our hearts, and calls to us.

Then he wants us to see our wretchedness and humbly to acknowledge it.

But he does not want us to go on like that;
> nor does he want us to keep accusing ourselves;
> and he does not want us to be overcome with misery about ourselves.

But he wants us hastily to *turn our attention to him.*

For he stands all alone, and waits for us, in mourning and sorrow, until we come. And he is waiting to receive us.

For we are his joy and his delight.

And he is our salvation and our life.

When I say "he stands all alone," I am not including the blessed company in heaven; but I mean his office and his working here on Earth.

Chapter 79

COMMENTARY

In this passage we find part of the answer given to Julian's prayer to experience contrition in an exemplary way. Contrition should be sincere, moderate, free of guilt-obsessions, and open to love.

A gentle but realistic counselor, Julian passes on to us advice about how to conduct ourselves when we are painfully aware of our sin. We become thus aware because God is calling to us.

But sin threatens to overcome us, if we keep on lamenting it.

There is a more profitable sight to lament, once we have been truthful about ourselves: it is the sight of Christ left alone because we no longer try to be partners in his work.

Christ here is like the father of the prodigal, whose son was his joy. And we are like that wayward child, who was starving for his father's love (Lk. 15:11–32).

Do Not Leave Him Alone

Where I say he waits for us, in sorrow and in mourning, that means all the true feeling of *contrition and compassion* we have within ourselves, and all the sorrow and mourning that we have because we are *not yet united to our Lord.*

All this is profitable.

It is Christ in us.

And though some of us feel it seldom, it departs never from Christ until he has brought us out of all our woe. For love is never without pity.

And when we fall into sin and forget about him and about the care of our own soul, then Christ acts alone in caring for us.

—And in this way he waits, in sorrow and in mourning. *Then it is up to us out of reverence and kindness to turn ourselves at once to our Lord and not to leave him alone.*

He is here for us alone; that is, only for us is he here. . . .But his goodness never permits us to be alone.

—But always he is with us.

—Tenderly, he excuses us.

—And ceaselessly he protects us from blame in his sight.

Chapter 80

COMMENTARY

Here we see how the prayer for the three in-depth experiences, or wounds, comes to be in Julian's ongoing journey: contrition, compassion, and desire to be united to God. The active presence of Christ within us brings these into being.

Christ enables us to have contrition and compassion.

Compassion is a favorite theme with Julian. She had prayed for compassion with Jesus in his pains. She experienced this to the point of regretting her petition. Then, in the thirteenth Showing, she shared not only in the reality of Christ's suffering as man, but, united with him, she felt compassion for those for whom, and in whom, he suffered. She was in part filled with compassion for all her even-Christians: "for that dear, dear people that shall be saved" (Chapter 28).

Prayer for Compassion

O God, when I have food, help me to remember the hungry; when I have work, help me to remember the jobless; when I have a comfortable home, help me to remember the homeless; when I am free of pain, help me to remember those who are ill. Destroy my complacency, bestir my compassion, that I may see in the needy the suffering face of Jesus Christ. (source unknown)

He Dwells Within Us

Our Lord showed himself many times reigning, but principally in the human soul.

—There is his place of rest and his noble city.

—From this noble see he will not go forth nor remove himself—ever.

—Marvellous and awe-inspiring is the place where our Lord dwells.

He wants us, therefore, *to give our attention* to his gracious touching:

—more enjoying in his holy love

—than sorrowing over our frequent fallings.

COMMENTARY

In the parable of the lord and the servant, the servant (Christ-Adam) was shown as a gardener (Chapter 51).

The ground which he cultivated was the whole of creation, especially that humanity which was to be restored and transformed.

Now the kingdom in which he reigns—in which he, by love, is the principle of order and fruitfulness—is like a glorious city. It is a city of joy.

The touchings of grace—the fleeting insights into what is in store for us—bring both repentance and joy.

But joy is to predominate.

What a simple and delightful way to pray: We sense God's presence and respond with joy.

Beholding God's Mercy

Here I understood that the Lord beholds the servant with
pity, and not with blame
>—for we are not asked in this passing life to live entirely
>without blame and sin.

He loves us endlessly, and we sin continually.
>—He shows us this very gently.
>—Then we sorrow and mourn with discretion
>>—turning to the *beholding of his mercy*
>>—holding fast to his love and goodness
>>—seeing that he is our medicine
>>—knowing that we do nothing [of ourselves] but sin.

And thus from the meekness that comes from the sight of
our sin
>—faithfully *knowing* his everlasting love
>—*thanking* him
>—and *praising* him, we please him. . . .

And all this was shown through spiritual understanding in
these blessed words: "I keep you ever safe."

Chapter 82

COMMENTARY

In recent years church and society have drawn our attention
to how we are implicated in the plight of the poor and the
marginalized. This sin is harder to deal with than our personal failings are.

In earlier years it seemed we could "give" to the poor, especially by living a simple lifestyle, and thus set right some
social injustices. The ascetic way could make right our social
sins.

But "we sin continually" because the poor are not an interest group in society with claims to be balanced against those
of other interest groups. The poor reveal the injustice in-
scribed in the whole social order:

Their marginalization harms them and, in a different way, damages the whole of society; it distorts society's perception of itself . . . creates an insensitive, hard-hearted, egotistical self-serving population, deaf to the voice of God.[2]

Racism and sexism are examples:

Thus, racism not only inflicts burdens on the despised race; it also generates in the majority a culture of contempt, injustice, violence that spills over into every aspect of their social and political life. Similarly, the subjugation of women not only inflicts injustices on the female part of the population; it also prompts men to adopt a false self-definition and embrace a love of domination that endangers society as a whole.[3]

Our personal sins build a prison which degrades and stunts society. But they can only be understood in relation to these social sins which paralyze us all, and make us blind and deaf as well.

When God, working through church and social thought, gently enlightens us on this point, and moves us to sorrow, then especially we need Julian's directives about how to mourn "with discretion." We need to offer prayers of thanking for this light. We need to persevere in prayers of beseeching, asking God to heal our deafness to the endangerment of society by sin.

Then we need to hear our Lord say that he loves that humanity for whom he is building his city. He looks on us "with pity, not with blame" because at the core of our being we are knit to him who took our common humanity.

Keeping a Balance

In the *beholding* of God we do not fall.
In the *beholding* of self we do not stand.
And both these are true, as I see it.
But *beholding our lord God* is the higher truth.
  —We are then much indebted to God for willing to
  show us this higher truth in this life.
I understood that while we are living here it is greatly to
our profit to behold both these truths together.
  —For the higher *beholding of our lord God* comforts our
  spirit and leads to true enjoyment in God.
  —the other—the lower beholding—keeps us in fear
  and makes us ashamed of ourselves.
But our good Lord wants us to keep ourselves more in the
beholding of the higher truth, without neglecting the lower, until such time as we shall be brought up above
  —where we shall have our lord Jesus as our *reward*,
  —and be *fulfilled* with joy and bliss without end.

Chapter 82

COMMENTARY

We are bound to lose our balance if we behold only the egotistical self, which is often blind, deaf, and paralyzed.

But in the *beholding* of God—in the center of our soul, in the
passion, and in the leading of the Holy Spirit—we find the
comfort and joy which enable us to put up patiently with
what we are of ourselves.

We are even to be *rewarded* for this penance which is built
into our life.

And we are to be completely filled with joy when the time
comes.

I Behold with Reverent Awe

I had, *in part,* touching, sight, and feeling of three properties of God, in which the strength and effect of the whole revelation resides. And they were seen in every Showing, and most particularly in the twelfth where it often says:

"It is I" [I am the One Who Is].

The properties are these: *life, love,* and *light.*

—The *life* is a marvelous intimacy.

—In *love* is gentle courtesy.

—In *light* is our nature enduring forever.

These properties are all one *goodness.*

—My own reason would be united to this *goodness* clinging to it with my whole strength.

I *beheld with reverent awe,* greatly marvelling in the sight, and in the feeling of sweet accord from our reason being in God,

—understanding that it is the highest gift we have received,

—and knowing that it is grounded in nature.

Our *faith* is a *light,* coming to us in nature from him who is our everlasting day, which is our father, God; in which *light* our mother Christ, and our good lord the Holy Ghost lead us in this passing life. . . .

The *light* is the cause of our life; the night is the cause of our pain and all our woe, by which we deserve reward and thanks from God.

With *mercy* and *grace,* we determine to know, and to believe in, this *light,* walking in it in *wisdom* and strength.

Chapter 83

COMMENTARY

"It is I," in the twelfth revelation (Chapter 26), is to be taken in solidarity with whatever meanings God gives to the individual. With Julian the insights into this truth were added to and renewed by touchings, sights, and feelings.

"It is I" is God making us aware of the divine presence, wisdom, and action in this—or—that reality, circumstance, or event—until we come to see that the being of God underlies all.

Whatever goodness there is, it is God.

—the *goodness* that is *life*, wherein God is closer to us than our clothing, or the interchange with a friend.

—the *goodness* that is *love*, which is the most joyous of our experiences.

—the *goodness* that is *light*:

—the mystery of God's sustaining us, as it was from the beginning with the separation of light from darkness.

—the mystery by which our Mother Christ, who is *mercy*, and our lord the Holy Ghost, who is *grace*, lead us on our pilgrimage.

In practice we find our way by faith, which accords with reason, which is grounded in nature.

All these touchings enhance our nature but do not replace or deny it.

—a *touch* energizes, activates, releases unrealized potential.

—what we *see* acts on us, through powers which are latent in the darkness.

—what we *feel* flows throughout our being.

These human experiences help us to recognize the spiritual senses of touch, sight, and feeling.

Measured by God's Wisdom

The *light* is *charity*, and it is measured out to us by *the wisdom of God* according to what most helps us.

—For the light is neither so bright that we can see our blessed day, nor is it completely hidden from us.

—But it is light in which we can live so as to be rewarded, deserving in our labor the endless thanks of God.

This was seen in the sixth Showing, where he said: "I thank you for your labor. . ." (Chapter 14).

I understood this *light* in three ways: the first is charity, uncreated; the second is charity which is created; and the third is charity which is given.

—Uncreated charity is God.

—Created charity is our soul in God.

—Charity given is virtue.

—And that is a gift of grace which is active in us, enabling us:

—to love God for himself;

—and to love ourselves, and all that God loves, for God.

Chapter 84

COMMENTARY

Surrounded by God's love we are able to live a life that is itself prayer, a life that will have its reward.

—In the sixth Showing, to which Julian refers, she saw heaven like a great feast, and beheld God's face like "a marvelous melody of endless love" (Chapter 14).

We have enough light to *behold*—to understand—that the nature of God is *love*; that God, through Christ, dwells in our soul by *love*; and that the action of God in our souls through the Holy Spirit, is *love*.

Thus, the Trinity is *love*: the maker, the keeper, the lover.

We may remember this *light* which is God, measured out to us according to our need.

Our need for this *light* which is God is greatest in times of darkness. We may remember this when we see the sensor lights on our streets—capable of light all along—turn on, and grow bright, as darkness closes in.

"You Are Blessed Indeed"

Notwithstanding our foolish living and our blindness here, yet endlessly our courteous Lord beholds us, *rejoicing* at the work of *grace* and *mercy* in our souls.

In all things we please him best by *wisely* and truly believing this and *rejoicing with God and in God.* . . .

For as surely as we shall be in the bliss of God without end, *praising and thanking,* just as surely have we always been in the foreknowledge of God, who loves us and knows us in the divine eternal purpose from without beginning. . . .

When the judgment comes and we are all brought up above, then we shall clearly see the mysteries that are now hidden from us.

Then none of us shall be moved to say in any way:

"Lord, if it had been thus and so, then all would have been well."

But we shall all say. . . :

"Lord you are blessed indeed! For it is this way, and it is well. And now we see indeed that everything is done as it was ordained before anything was made."

Chapter 85

COMMENTARY

Thanking takes the form of enjoying and praising and blessing what God is and what God does.

We may reflect on *blessing* God by recalling its opposite, which is cursing:

—the one who attempts to place a *curse* on God's workings would, if it were possible, blast out of existence all that seems displeasing to oneself.

—the one who *blesses* affirms and rejoices in what God does.

We offer a *blessing* to one another, or receive a *blessing* in religious worship, to invoke God's favor.

We pronounce God *blessed* to acknowledge God's favor and goodness.

Yet, given our human condition, though we do not curse God with those who contemn Divine power, we stand in confusion and questioning before what does not seem right to us in this creation.

So *thanking*, blessing God, is an act of faith.

Thanking in heaven will be undergirded with a new kind of *knowing* indeed: we will then know that all things are well, and see for ourselves why that is so.

"I Am the Ground of Your Praying"

Let us all together *pray to God* for charity, with God working in us
—*thanking,*
—*trusting,*
—*rejoicing.*
For this is how our Lord wants us to pray, according to the way I understood his meaning in all the Showings, and especially in those sweet words where he says merrily:
"I am the ground of your praying."
For truly I saw and understood that the reason why our Lord showed it was that he wants it to be known and understood better than it is.
When we know this, he will give us grace to love him and to hold fast to him.

Chapter 86

COMMENTARY
Who should pray? All of us together.
—sometimes, visibly together;
—always, in invisible union with those who pray.
For what should we pray? for charity—for love.
—that love which is God
—that love which is the ongoing union of the core of our soul with Christ, and through him with the Trinity, and with our even-Christians.
—that love which should come to permeate our lives:
—in what we do
—in what we desire
—in the way we understand God, ourselves, and all that God loves.
We pray to eliminate the obstacles to love—the paralysis, the blindness, the deafness, and all that leads to sin.
How can we pray? Because the ground of our beseeching is Christ.

This is the sum total of our *beseeching*, by which our will is in accord with God's will.

Beholding this, we rejoice. In our prayer of *thanking*, we know inwardly, each day anew, the centrality of love.

Because Christ is the *ground* of our *beseeching*, we *trust*. Here, too, is *beholding*: knowing what love is, thanking God for it and rejoicing in it.

All these will be ever new, as the evolution of the world requires new shapes for love.

For Christ is the ground from which each new prayer arises, and in whom the fruit of prayer is realized and rooted.

Such is the theme of these lines from the epistle to the Ephesians (3:14–19):

> I kneel before the Father ... that he may grant you in accord with the riches of his glory to be strengthened with power through the Spirit in the inner self, and that Christ may dwell in your hearts through faith; that you, rooted and grounded in love, may have strength to comprehend with all the holy ones what is the breadth and length and height and depth, and to know the love of Christ that surpasses knowledge, so that you may be filled with all the fullness of God.

"Learn It Well"

Ever after the time of the Showings, I often desired to know what was our Lord's meaning.

After more than fifteen years, I was answered by a spiritual understanding in these words:

"Do you want to know your Lord's meaning in all this?
Learn it well: Love was its meaning.

"Who showed it to you? Love.

"What did he show you? Love.

"Why did he show it to you? for Love.

"Hold firmly to this, and you shall understand Love ever more and more.

"But you will never know nor learn any other thing
— only love."

And in this way I was taught that *love* was our Lord's meaning.

Chapter 86

COMMENTARY

Julian describes here, it seems, her prayer of silent beseeching, simply desiring of God to understand the Showings. The answer was long in coming.

Even for Julian, with her whole-hearted giving of self to God, spiritual understanding came long after the right words had been heard and repeated. Even the powerful experience of the sixteen Showings, given in a period of a few hours, did not fully come together for her for over fifteen years. For some five years more she reflected and prayed. Then love became the answer to her "who," and "what," and "why."

To pray always means here to *beseech* God until the gift we seek is given. Then we can *behold* the gift of this deeper understanding, *thanking* God. In this way those who are not acclaimed as wise arrive at spiritual wisdom and are at rest.

Teach me, O God, the meaning of love.

Afterword

A Schema on Prayer in the Showings
Julian teaches us about prayer in the context of how we live our life: she does not present prayer as a system but as the experience of God. She draws on her experiences and on those of others.

We may now look back and see this teaching as a whole.

This is an overview of that teaching.

Beseeching and Thanking: God Follows Us
Prayer generally means beseeching for, or desiring, God. Prayer, if it could, would bring us heaven on Earth. We can pray always in our desire for the goodness that is God. Thanking is connected with prayer, for when we understand God's gifts and activities, we are drawn to do what God wants and to find enjoyment in God's ways and to express our praise. We come to realize that God also thanks us, rewarding us and giving us gifts beyond what we could ever deserve.

This beseeching is founded realistically in our earthly life, for God comes down to the lowest part of our need. Hence, we can pray for whatever we need, remembering that God is the goodness in all things. We direct our prayer to that divine goodness. We turn to the prayer of beseeching because our nature makes us long for the happiness that is God. We trust to have this desire fulfilled, whatever form it takes in our lives, because our prayer springs from Christ, who is the ground, the foundation of our praying: Christ enables us to pray.

We are, nonetheless, partners with God, in the deed that is being done, in helping form that city which is where God reigns. As partners with God we learn compassion by keeping before us a sweet remembrance of the passion. Above all, we pray, in union with others, for charity, for love: for God who creates us, restores us, and shapes our lives by the Holy Spirit. Here, thanking shares in the wisdom of God who will make all things well. In heaven *thanking* breaks out in eternal praise and in an overflow of joy when we at last know that indeed all things are well.

In our beseeching, God follows us, helping us in our need. For our comfort, let us remember that this seeking is as good as beholding, as finding.

This is what Julian sums up in her definition of prayer:

Prayer is a *right understanding* of the fullness of joy that is to come

—with intense longing

—and unwavering trust.

Falling short of the joy that we are by nature ordained to

—makes us to *long.*

True *understanding* and *love*, with a sweet *remembrance* of our Savior, by *grace*

—makes us to *trust.*

Prayer takes the form of *beseeching*, a new, gracious, lasting will of the soul, united and fastened to our Lord's will by the sweet working of the Holy Spirit.

Thanking understands and rejoices in part in what is being done: *Thanking* is a new, inward knowing, accompanied with great reverence and loving awe, inclining us to do with all our strength what God draws us toward and inwardly to give thanks and enjoy. It is eternally new.

Prayer of Beholding: We Follow God

In *beholding*, our powers are fixed on God, with understanding and love, or on our self in God. Here, *we follow God.* Julian records many forms of *beholding* which God granted to her, where she followed God. God touched her, opened her spiritual eye, and made her feel the divine presence as life, light, and love—all properties of one *goodness*. Above all, she beheld the Trinity in the Christ-Mother. Jesus, familiar and awe-inspiring, is her divine friend.

We follow God who says to us "I It am," as divine presence active in all and as the being of all and as beyond all. Thus God is both ultimate reality and ultimate mystery.

We follow God when we see our self revealed, both the weak, sinful self and the true self, the center of our being in which God dwells. This is the city now building:

Beholding this while we are here is most pleasing to God and benefits us. It makes the soul that beholds it desire to become like to him whom it beholds; and through grace it unites the soul to God in rest and peace.

Julian's definition of prayer applies here, too, for the one who beholds God thus, shares in Christ's spiritual thirst and desires an ever-more-complete union.

Whether prayer is silent and totally inward, or whether it is in words formed interiorly, or whether it breaks out in speech are not important dividing lines in Julian's teaching. Her approach underscores how totally human her prayer is, whether as beseeching and thanking, or as beholding.

But, whether God follows us, or we follow God—in the deepest sense, God does all. And love is God's meaning.

Notes

Introduction
1. Adapted in part from Jean Leclercq, *The Love of Learning and the Desire for God* (New York: Mentor Omega Books, 1960), especially pp. 22-26, 79-80.

Beginnings
1. Leo J. O'Donovan, "Karl Rahner, S.J. (1904-1984). In Memoriam," *Cross Currents* 34 (Summer 1984): 211-212.

The Focus of Prayer: The Goodness of God
1. Jessica Powers, *Selected Poetry of Jessica Powers,* Regina Siegfried and Robert Morneau, eds. (Kansas City: Sheed and Ward, 1989), p. 21.
2. Julian may have related this image of the lace point which she in all likelihood knew about or even produced. In this way of imaging the same point is everywhere creating a pattern that is one and many.

    Some mystics think of the soul as a mirror in which God, like a beam of light, comes into focus in the center of the soul and radiates from that bright center. There are many other ways of understanding this metaphor of the point.
3. Ireneus, *Adv. Haer.* V, 6.1., *Sources Chrétiennes,* 153, pp. 72-81, as cited by Leonardo Boff, *Trinity and Society* (Maryknoll, N.Y.: Orbis Books, 1988), p. 26.

Christ the Center of Prayer
1. Bede Griffiths, "Christianity in the Light of the East," *Bulletin of the North American Board for East-West Dialogue* (October 1989): 8.

2. "Because there is no specific connection of the canticle in the context of Mary's pregnancy and her visit to Elizabeth, the Magnificat [with the possible exception of verse 48] may have been a Jewish-Christian hymn that Luke found appropriate at this point of his story. Even if not composed by Luke, it fits in well with themes found elsewhere in Lk...." The *Catholic Study Bible*, ed. Donald Senior et al. (New York: Oxford University Press, 1990), p. 99, footnote, I, 46-55.
3. The Paris manuscript of the Showings has "true" rather than "new." But "new" (as in the Sloane manuscript) seems appropriate here, suggesting the moment-by-moment working of grace. It may recall St. Augustine who exclaims in the *Confessions*: "O beauty! Ever ancient and ever new!" (10:27). It also suggests the Scripture text: "Behold, I make all things new" (Rev. 21:5).
4. From "The Moment" by Edwina Gateley, *Psalms for a Laywoman* (Trabuco Canyon, Cal.: Source Books, 1987), p. 15. First published in Great Britain in 1986 by Anthony Clarke, Herefordshire, England.
5. Ann Adkins, "Life is what happens when we are making other plans," *The Roll* V-VI (Sept. 3, 1989): 84-86.
6. Brant Pelphrey, *Christ our Mother: Julian of Norwich* (The Way of the Christian Mystics Series), Vol. 7 (Wilmington, Del.: Michael Glazier, 1989), p. 160.

Christ the Foundation of Prayer
1. The "divine will" is not an erratic whim or an arbitrary show of power imposed on the creature. Rather, it unfolds by God's interaction with the freedom that is integral to beings acting in accord with their natures.
2. E. I. Watkin, *On Julian of Norwich, and in Defense of Margery Kempe* (Exeter: University of Exeter, 1979), p. 30.
3. E.I. Watkin, p. 31.
4. Jessica Powers, "The Place of Splendor," in *Selected Poetry of Jessica Powers*, p. 123.
5. Ritamary Bradley, "Perception of Self in Julian of Norwich's *Showings*," *Downside Review* (July 1986): 238, adapted in

part from Bernard T. Smith, "Paul, Mystic and Missionary," *Journal of Dharma* (Sept. 1981): 433.

6. Gregory Baum, "The Witness of Etty Hillesum," *Ecumenist* (Jan.-Feb. 1985): 25.

7. Jessica Powers, "The Great Mystery," in *Selected Poetry of Jessica Powers*, p. 100.

8. Janet Morley, *All Desires Known* (London: SPCK, 1992), p. 26.

9. Gregory Baum, "The Witness of Etty Hillesum": 27.

The Height and Depth of Julian's Prayer

1. Gregory Baum, "The Witness of Etty Hillesum": 27.

2. Gregory Baum, "Sociology and Salvation," *Theological Studies* 50 (Dec. 1989): 736.

3. Baum, "Sociology and Salvation": 736.